A remarkable book about a remarkable man.

—James Leedy, Archivist
Bluefield State College

Dr. Henry Lake Dickason <u>was</u> somebody. This account of his life is necessary reading – not just for the story of a life well-lived but for the larger story of African Americans struggling to better their lot in a world of Jim Crow where the odds were against them. Crabtree's well-researched and, above all, sensitive narrative of Dickason's journey evokes the warmth of family, the love of place, and the depths of a young man's striving soul.

—Vicki Lane
author of the Elizabeth Goodweather Mysteries

This is the fascinating and fast-paced story of the grandson of slaves whose career was devoted to the Bluefield Colored Institute, later to morph from a high school to the Bluefield State College. "Lake" was encouraged by his father, also his teacher in a one-room log school, to attend Bluefield where a high school education was available to black students. Eventually he met a math teach who encouraged him to work for a degree at Ohio State so he could return and teach, and also to marry her! The story follows the triumphs and tragedies of schoolwork as well as family life at a time when tuberculosis and infection were difficult to cure.

Becky Crabtree has thoroughly documented this historical novel with 55 illustrations ranging from vintage photos, to college archives, to newspaper articles, to handwritten letters. These cover Dickason's entire life from 1886-1957 and talk about his encounters with such diverse notables, as Leontyne Price, Thurgood Marshall, Count Bassie and Eleanor Roosevelt! Also included are the influences of William Du Bois and Booker T. Washington on educational philosophy. Dickason's life is set in the border county of Monroe, one of the most beautiful rural areas in West Virginia.

—Fred Zeigler, President
Monroe County (WV) Historical Society

This book brought back memories of my younger years and school times. These were struggling years for the Negro youth as we had no high school for the Negros. There was a small Negro community in our area of very good Negro people. Dr. Dickason's family was among them. After the law passed, they could go to school with the white children. Many of them did. Becky did a wonderful job of capturing their lives in this book. I really enjoyed reading it.

I met Dr. Dickason, but I knew Mrs. Flossie quite well. She was a spirited lady. She gave our church apples from their orchard every year to make apple butter for sale.

Most of the ones in this area have passed on. The younger ones have moved away, but many of them come back and visit from time to time.

—William S. Broyles
Lindside Resident and Broyles Funeral Home Director, retired

Informative about the hardships black people faces in the late 1800s and early 1900s. One was education.

—Monnie Raines Martin

Becky has done a wonderful job on the book of the life of Lake Dickason. I was born and raised in the village of Lindside. I did not know Lake as I grew up but can remember people talking about him. He was greatly admired by everyone in our community. After Lake passed away, Flossie moved back to Lindside and we became friends. Flossie was a well-educated lady and her thoughts and ideals were a little different from most of the people in our community. I am truly blessed to have called her my friend.

—Sara "Susie" Ballard Wickline
Lindside, West Virginia resident

Try and Be Somebody

The Story of Dr. Henry Lake Dickason

for Margie
& Robert,
Hope you
enjoy!

Becky Crabtree

Also by Becky Hatcher Crabtree
Alaska Hoops: Tales from the Girls' Locker Room
Drunk on Peace and Quiet
Hung Over with Grandma

Try and Be Somebody

The Story of Dr. Henry Lake Dickason

Becky Hatcher Crabtree

with Merri Jackson Hess

Fathom Publishing Company

Disclaimer

All the people, places, and dates in this book are as real as can be. Events such as church homecomings and sitting on the porch are those common to the era and would have likely taken place. The thoughts and conversations of the characters are based solely on the author's vivid imagination influenced by those who knew the Dickason family.

Library of Congress Control Number: 2017951677

ISBN 978-1-888215-29-8 (Trade cloth)
ISBN 978-1-888215-30-4 (Paperback)
Ebook ISBN 978-1-888215-31-1(Kindle edition)
Ebook ISBN 978-1-888215-32-8 (ePub edition)

www.beckycrabtree.com

www.fathompublishing.com
Fathom Publishing Company
P.O. Box 200448
Anchorage, Alaska 99520-0448
Telephone /Fax 907-272-3305
Printed in the United States of America

"The truth is not a bidimensional thing; it's not flat. It's rounded; it's like a sphere, so there's always a hidden face. There's one that is revealed because there's light reflecting on it, but there's always a hidden one, and once you go around to see the hidden one, it moves, and that's life."

—Edgar Ramirez

Dedicated to all children,
especially those in the mountains
of southern West Virginia,
in hopes that they find
the power of their dreams
to overcome obstacles.

Every great dream begins with a dreamer. Always remember, you have within you the strength, the patience, and the passion to reach for the stars to change the world.

—Harriet Tubman

Success in life is founded upon attention to the small things rather than to the large things; to the every day things nearest to us rather than to the things that are remote and uncommon.

—Booker T. Washington

Table of Contents

List of Illustrations

Key Dates

1827	Raeburn Hall Dickason born
1883	Mary Fannie Ross Dickason married Guy R. Dickason
1885	Hattie M. Dickason born
1886	Henry Lake Dickason born
	Delbert Fleshman Dunlap born
1895	Raburn Sidney Dickason born
	Hattie M. Dickason died
1896	Bluefield Colored Institute opened
1899	Bernard French Dickason born
1903	Henry Lake Dickason goes to Bluefield Colored Institute
1905	W.E.B. Du Bois "Men of Niagara" speech
1905-6	Booker T. Washington raised funds to finance Tuskegee Institute
1906	Henry Lake Dickason's graduation from Bluefield Colored Institute
1907	Raeburn Hall Dickason dies
1910	Henry Lake Dickason graduated from Bluefield Colored Institute Normal School
1913	Henry Lake Dickason's graduation from The Ohio State University B.A.
	Henry Lake Dickason elected General Secretary of National Alpha Phi Alpha
1914	Henry Lake Dickason graduated from The Ohio State University M.A.
	Henry Lake Dickason and Grace Ethel Robinson marry
	Henry Lake Dickason's first year teaching at Bluefield Colored Institute
	Henry Lake Dickason elected General President of National Alpha Phi Alpha
1915	Henry Lake Dickason, Jr. born and died
1917	Delbert Fleshman Dunlap starts teaching at Bluefield Colored Institute
1918	End of World War I
1919	Grace E. Robinson Dickason died
1923	Henry Lake Dickason promoted to vice-principal of Bluefield Colored Institute
	Bernard French Dickason admitted to sanitarium
	Bernard French Dickason died
1926	Booker T. Washington addressed Bluefield Colored Institute graduating class
	Raburn Sidney Dickason died

1929	Guy R. Dickason died
1931	Henry Lake Dickason became Dean Dickason
	Bluefield Colored Institute name changed to Bluefield State Teachers College
1932	Alpha Phi Alpha in 1932, the first fraternity organized at Bluefield State
	Henry Lake Dickason and Flossie Mack married
1933	Mary Fannie Ross Dickason died
1935	Robert Andrew Dickason born
1936	Dr. Robert P. Sims demoted to business manager at Bluefield Colored Institute
	Henry Lake Dickason appointed acting president of Bluefield Colored Institute by the State Board of Education
1937	Bluefield Colored Institute campus fire
1938	Arter Hall and new gymnasium completed at Bluefield Colored Institute
	Henry Lake Dickason became Appointed President of Bluefield Colored Institute
	Henry Lake Dickason traveled to New Orleans and spoke at Alpha Phi Alpha convention
1939	Robert Andrew Dickason adopted by Lake and Flossie Dickason
1939-45	World War II
1940	Library Wing added to Conley Hall, Mahood Hall, Payne Hall, and faculty housing built on BSC campus
1940-51	Henry Lake Dickason served on the Bluefield City's Draft Board
1942	Henry Lake Dickason awarded honorary Doctorate of Pedagogy, Virginia State College
1943	Bluefield Colored Institute name changed to Bluefield State College
1945	Bluefield State College 50th anniversary
1948	Henry Lake Dickason awarded West Virginia State College, Doctor of Literary Law
1949	Bluefield State College met the requirements of the North Central Association and granted full accreditation
1950	Technical Education Building added to BSC campus, later called Dickason Hall
1952	Henry Lake Dickason retired from Bluefield State College
1953	Henry Lake Dickason appointed to serve on the board of the Greenbrier-Monroe County Tuberculosis and Health Association
	Henry Lake Dickason went to Morristown College in Morristown, Tennessee
1957	Henry Lake Dickason died
1958	Delbert Fleshman Dunlap died
1978	Flossie Mack Dickason died
2016	West Virginia Historical Marker for Henry Lake Dickason installed

In everyone's life, at some time, our inner fire goes out. It is then burst into flame by an encounter with another human being. We should all be thankful for those people who rekindle the inner spirit.

—Albert Schweitzer

Acknowledgements

First, I must thank my dearest friend, Merri Jackson Hess, for sharing the obsession of Henry Lake Dickason with me over the last two years. We've traveled to places important to telling the story of Dr. Dickason's life and spent hours on the phone choosing words and digesting ideas about the era in which he lived.

My teacher and editor, Jay St. Vincent, never wavered in her support of this story. Her mantra was, "Keep writing. It is important." She didn't waver in her support of proper grammar and punctuation, either. As is true about my other writings, this wouldn't've (Is that a word?!) happened without her.

Connie Taylor, at Fathom Publishing, makes book publishing much easier and faster than it could be and does it with kindness.

Many were gracious in their encouragement and willingness to discuss with me their first-hand experiences with Dr. Dickason, especially Mr. Ergie Smith, Mrs. Mary B. Ross, and Mrs. Merilyn Booth Fleshman. Mrs. Dorothy M. Craft filled in colorful details of long-ago life at the school. Mrs. Joyce Perry explained away my confusion about Bluefield Hardware and Bluefield Supply. Janet Jackson helped me find the AME Church in Gap Mills.

Dr. William Robertson added his life-changing encounter with Dr. Dickason, and in doing so, told a great deal about both men.

Mr. William Broyles spoke to Dr. Dickason as a child and formed an opinion so respectful that he remembered it for seventy years. He was also a neighbor of Flossie Dickason after Dr. Dickason's death and told leg-slapping stories about her managing the farm. He owns the property containing the Dickason Family Cemetery and has been more than generous allowing me to visit it. Cynthia Morris, his daughter and her husband Sterl, took us up on the mountain to locate the cemetery where fascination set in.

Mrs. Bobbie Jean Spangler Comer told impressive tales from her childhood meetings of Dr. Dickason.

The members of the Bluefield State College Alumni Association, led by Deidre Guyton, were generous in sharing knowledge and encouragement. The president of Bluefield State, Dr. Marsha V. Krotseng, was also gracious in allowing us to use images and text from the school's centennial yearbook.

Monnie Raines Martin and Nedra Pendleton Shaver, co-authors of ***A Glimpse into Lindside Area Schools: Monroe County, West Virginia***, provided well-researched historical materials for this book. Local historians Alice Bradley, Susie Wickline, Sarah Shires, Betty Spangler, and Sam Shires told me stories of the Lindside Dickasons that found their way into this biography.

Dr. Craig Mohler allowed use of priceless glimmers of history found only in our long-running weekly newspaper, The Monroe Watchman of Union, West Virginia.

Mr. James Leedy at the Bluefield State College Archives worked overtime to find images and text for this project. He is a jewel of a gentleman.

Vanni Prichard edited with a careful eye and found mistakes I had missed a dozen times. Her work made this story better.

The Peters Mountain DAR sponsored a historic marker to honor Dr. Dickason that provided a springboard of knowledge to start writing. Thank you to my DAR friends, especially Faye Ramsey.

Roger Crabtree put up with quite a bit as I pounded my pillow and stared at the computer screen and walked in the woods listening for Dr. Dickason's voice. As always, he had enough patience and sanity to replenish mine.

Finally, I thank the fresh faces and voices of our grandchildren Isabel, Elizabeth, Clark, Gabriel, and Rachel Una who help me realize how much the world has changed and yet stays the same. May their lives have enough to overcome to make them strong and may they recognize those sleeping dragons of injustice and slay them as often as necessary.

Becky Hatcher Crabtree
September 2017

Introduction

I thank everyone who assisted in my development. I realize that I owe so much to so many. God truly blessed me with loving parents, outstanding teachers and others who have contributed to my life's journey. In addition to being a husband and father, I have served as a teacher, coach, school administrator, consultant, diplomat, camp founder, college official and fund raiser. I have worked for a governor, been a four-time presidential appointee, and represented the United States in 65 countries around the world and am the recipient of numerous awards and several honorary doctorate degrees. I have "tried to be somebody."

The question has been posed many times, has there been a time or person you deem pivotal to your journey? The answer comes forth loudly in the affirmative. After all these years, I remember the day and person who changed my life forever.

I shall never forget that hot late August day in 1950. It had finally arrived. It was the day I was to leave for Bluefield State College. The second oldest of eight children, my father and mother were sacrificing so very much to send me to college for four years. Monies that were needed for the family at home would be diverted to this endeavor. My father and I discussed this as we walked to the Roanoke, Virginia, Norfolk and Western train station. Even though it was going to be a difficult time for him financially, I could feel the sense of pride my father felt. His son was off to college. After a two and one-half hour train ride, I arrived in Bluefield and went directly to the college's administration building.

It was there on that day that my hopes and dreams seemed doomed and destined for the scrap heap. I felt a sense of loss and loneliness that afternoon. All the time and effort put into this venture for nothing were uppermost in my mind. Even with all the pennies my family and I had scraped together, I did not have enough to enroll.

Then something providential happened. The storm abated and an angel appeared in the person of the President of the college. Dr. Henry Lake Dickson entered my life.

This is a gripping biography that should have been written years ago. Peruse this work by Becky Crabtree and be introduced to an outstanding individual, Dr. Henry Lake Dickason. See how he guides and directs people to lofty heights. Watch as he lifts Bluefield State College to a position of prominence. Read how he changes my life immediately and inspires me to "try to be somebody".

William B. Robertson

Proud graduate of Bluefield State College – 1954 & 1956.

September 18, 2017

Part I

Chapter 1 – Delicious

Lake's favorite memory was sitting on the edge of the front porch of his family's home, swinging his dusty, dark feet back and forth as he watched the October sun set. The sky was a brilliant pink with purple streaks that evening. It must've been 1892 because he had just turned six years old the month before. Momma had made a molasses cake for his birthday and sprinkled it with powdered sugar and Uncle Hugh had given him a black and white foxhound pup. He had wanted to be six years old as long as he could remember because then he would get to go to the little log school down the mountain.

The nights were getting cooler and the first brilliant colors were starting to show on trees all over the mountain. Chestnut trees glowed bright yellow and sugar trees were changing to a fiery red. The ash trees and the black walnuts had already lost their golden slivers of leaves and the small dogwoods and huge Spanish Oaks were turning ruby red. The Black and White Oaks would turn red, too, but they held onto their leaves longer than the other trees. Momma said it was like the mountain was dressing up for one last dance before winter.

After supper and chores, he sat on the porch swinging his legs and cuddling the puppy in the lap of his rough cotton pants. His mamma was stringing and breaking beans, pop-pop-pop in the old rocking chair behind him. Whippoorwills called across the valleys to one another. Tobacco smoke from Papa's pipe drifted into the crisp air. The tobacco smell was so strong that Lake could almost taste it.

Papa held the pipe in one hand and blew smoke in a long steady stream. "We'll start up school when I get all the apples stored and some more wood in," he announced, "I guess Lake is big enough to come this year." He replaced the pipe in his mouth and smiled at his son with the pipe stem between his teeth. Lake had turned around when he heard the word "school."

Papa and Momma started singing bits of old hymns together and laughing. It had been a while since he had heard them laugh; they worried a lot about his sickly older sister. Hattie was sleeping inside the cabin and tonight there was no coughing.

The colors of the sunset faded away and the sky darkened. Stars started to twinkle into view. Lake leaned his head and shoulder against the porch post beside him and listened to the night sounds. Cricket chirps were slowing down in the cool and the old screech owl was nearby practicing his funny whoo-whoo-whoo sounds. It was still warm enough for a stray mosquito though and Lake swatted at one he heard buzzing near his face. The movement of his arm jiggled his body and the sleeping dog stretched a little, looked at Lake and yawned, then went back to sleep.

It was a delicious time, full of beauty and love and excitement for the future. Lake was nearly asleep himself when the strong arms of his father scooped him up and carried him to bed. He didn't realize it but his mom had already plucked the puppy off his lap and carried it off to its bed in the kindling box on the porch. She didn't allow dogs inside.

His world was perfect that evening, his best childhood recollection. It was a long time before things felt perfect again.

Chapter 2 – School

The most thrilling part of Lake's life up until then was looking forward to going to school. He had learned a lot at home, how to write his letters and a few dozen words, but he shivered with anticipation when he thought about getting to learn more. His mom packed a biscuit with apple butter wrapped in a piece of cloth and a big golden apple in his lunch bucket. Hattie told him that he could get a drink at the back of the schoolroom. A bucket filled with cool water from the spring sat there, she informed him.

Hattie thought she knew everything because she had gone to Chestnut Grove School the last school term. It seemed to give her the right to boss him around. Even though she coughed a lot and wasn't much fun to play with, he decided to listen to her because he wanted to be the best student there. Lake wasn't going to take a chance on missing something. Hattie must have told him a dozen times, "You sit still when others are telling Pa their lessons and raise yo' hand if you have something to say and it better be important." Lake would nod yes every time she said it. "And don't pay attention to the big boys. They call everybody names and tease and if you pay them no mind, they quit."

His father was the teacher. Even though Guy Dickason had spent hours cleaning and readying the one room school during the fall, he left earlier on the first day than his children because he needed a few minutes for last minute preparations. He also needed a moment to himself to gather his own thoughts. It was hard farming over a hundred acres and teaching school, working in the fields until late and then, after supper, studying until bedtime. This year Hattie and Lake would be students. Guy worried about Hattie's health and about Lake concentrating. He felt Lake was smart and he hoped that he would understand the importance of getting an education.

He put his hands together, elbows on the desk and prayed before the children arrived.

On the first day of school, Hattie and Lake got up while it was still dark, washed their faces, got dressed quickly, and did their chores. Both had jobs to do, but Lake thought there might be less to do when school started. He was surprised when he still had to carry feed and water to the chickens before school and fill the kindling box by the cook stove so Mama could build a fire to cook during the day. "Chickens don't take the day off from eating, do they?" his mother was stern when Lake questioned having to carry corn to them on a school day. Then she turned away so he wouldn't see her smile.

The children followed the path to the road, turned left and walked south for a half mile on the narrow dirt road then followed another path that cut down through the woods to the school. Hattie coughed as she got warm from walking, but she cooled off in the woods going downhill.

Years before, Jacob Dickason and Rev. Parker Lucas, from across the mountain in Giles County, built a one-room log church. The logs used to build it were so huge that it only took six of them for the entire building and earned it the name, 'Six-Log Church.' Lake and Hattie's grandfather, Raeburn, knew other slaves who helped build it. "Massa' Jacob taught all his slaves to read," Raeburn told the children, "even if it was agin the law, but as quick as it was legal, in 1865, he wanted all the young'uns on this mountain to have a place for schoolin' and the church became a school."

He told stories about the "olden days" and explained that Dickason wasn't really their name; it was the name of the family that owned them. "I can't say what our last name really is, chil'run, because it has been lost." Then he looked at the sky and his face grew sad. He sighed before he went on. "Before I was called Dickason, I was called Hall because my massa' — that's what we called the man who owned us — was Massa' Hall." Then he'd brighten up at the next part in the story every time he told it. He'd slap his leg and tell about the time when Jacob bought him, "I told Massa' Jacob, right there on the auction block, if he upped the $1500 bid that no good man from Georgia was offering, to $1700, I'd pay the difference. And Master Jacob did! And I did! $200! Took me three years, but by cracky, it was shore worth it to stay in these mountains!" Lake would shake his head every time he heard this story and wonder how his grandpa could be so bold. *How could he stand in front of people, chained to a post and still talk sense to the men bidding on him?* Lake was in awe of his grandpa.

Raeburn could do almost anything on the farm; he cut down trees and made boards, tended cattle, planted crops, cut hay, built barns, threshed wheat, and killed hogs, but his main job was to build wagons. His honesty and work ethic was legendary on the mountain and even at 62 years old, he worked hard in the fields every day.

One hot afternoon as Raeburn, Guy, and Lake were all making hay shocks with pitchforks, Lake was working slowly. The hay was prickly and his arms were tired and he was miserable enough to make grumbling sounds but not brave enough to look up and complain. His daddy stopped working and leaned on his pitchfork wiping his face with his handkerchief, "It takes hard work to get ahead," he said gently. "Your grandfather and grandmother and your mother and I have always worked hard so you can have more than us. You must always do your best, too."

Only known photo of Henry Lake Dickason's grandfather: Raeburn Hall Dickason, slave, wagon builder and freedman farmer, 1827-1907. A Glimpse into Lindside Area Schools, Monroe County, West Virginia, Monnie Raines Martin and Nedra Pendleton Shaver.

Lake could hear his papa take a deep breath and wiped his face again. Raeburn walked up and stared at Lake. The boy was shamed and afraid of what Raeburn would say.

It was a soft vapor of a voice, "Child, you must do it on your own. No one is going to offer you more strength than what you and the good Lord can do together. You gotta dig down deep inside here." Raeburn touched the little boy's chest almost as lightly as he spoke.

The men were solemn and Raeburn added, "It makes a lot of difference when the land you work is your own and you sweat working beside your own blood kin, making a future for them. Heaven, boys, heaven, no matter how hot it is."

The men's words washed over him, erased his fear, and made him feel like he could and should do great things. He brushed the stray bits of hay off his neck and shook his arms out and got back to work at a good pace. They all went back to work and had the hay shocked by suppertime.

That night as Lake lay awake listening to a summer storm roar on Peters Mountain, he felt proud that they had beat the rain and thought maybe that his effort had helped. His parents did work hard, everybody he knew on the mountain did. If it felt this good to work hard, Lake made a promise to himself that he would always try a little harder and work a little longer than he first thought he could.

That's what Lake intended to do from the first step he took on the worn path his first morning of school, to be the best and make his daddy and momma and grandpa proud. He intended to look everyone there in the eye and tell them *"Good Morning"* like his mother told him to do and to be kind to others who needed help. Hattie had laughed at that and said, "Won't anybody need more help than you, Lake!"

Lessons began with the young ones going first and reciting the alphabet together. Lake got moved back to the second bench and worked with students who were a little older. He was glad to sit beside his cousin Raburn Sidney, too. Both the boys paid attention and didn't take part in the foolishness that started in the back rows every now and then.

School wasn't easy and his papa expected more than Lake realized when he had looked forward to school. The wooden benches were hard, too, but he completely forgot about that when he was figuring out a word or looking at a map.

At the end of the day, he left Hattie in the schoolyard and ran all the way home to tell his momma about the day. She sat on the porch and listened and laughed and Lake felt grown up telling Momma about school. "Run along now and change into play clothes," she said when his talking slowed down, "I've got to finish supper so it's ready when your Papa gets here. And you have hogs and chickens to feed and Bessie needs to be in the barn so I can milk. Scat, now."

Lake practically strutted to hang up his school clothes and get to work.

Chapter 3 – Stories

Lake could read some even before he started to school and he thought he was smart enough. His momma always told him so, not out loud, but in little ways like the way she smiled at him when he told stories about the world outside of the mountain and when she served him a bigger piece of pie "because he needed to grow his brain some more."

Papa had given him a faded *Swinton's Third Reader* to use and he kept it clean and dry in a sack his momma had made from an old apron. She left the strings on it so he could carry it over his shoulder.

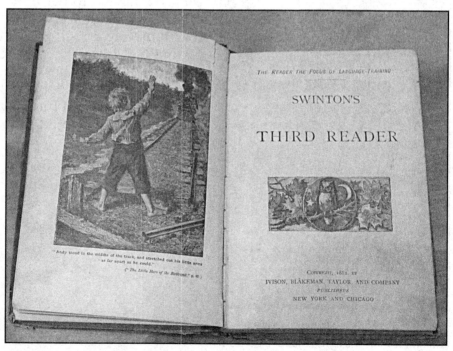

Swinton's Third Reader was Lake's proud possession. Becky Crabtree.

He was real proud of having his own book and took special care of it. He could tell that she was proud of it, too, by the way she ran her fingers down the front cover and turned the pages gentle-like as if they were butterfly wings. His momma could read, too, but she didn't have much time to spend on it. There was always cooking and washing to do.

Sometimes, she asked him to read to her while she was at the stove or cleaning up the dishes. That reading book had stories of places and people that Lake had not known about. Every new story became his favorite. He read about a bird that could talk, a gray parrot, and wondered what the birds on the mountain would say if they could talk. That story had some big new words in it, but he practiced and practiced reading it until he was allowed to go on. Then he read about Daniel Webster and then a place called Norway and after that, a girl who lived in a lighthouse. They gave him a lot of new things to think about. There were stories about familiar things, too, about nut cracking and having a pet squirrel,

and turning a grindstone. Every night, he sat at the table while his mother cooked and read to her until his father came in from the fields. At first he read it with his finger tracing the words until his mother asked, "Is there an eye in that finger?" and they both laughed. Then he held the book tightly with both hands and read hungrily, his dark eyes darting from word to word.

In Swinton's Reader, one story told of a little girl who lit the lights that shined from her home, a lighthouse. Becky Crabtree.

Chapter 4 – Homecomings

Church gatherings were almost as much fun for Lake as school, especially homecomings. His family attended the Dickason Chapel, a log building less than a mile away near Chestnut Grove School. The church hosted two wonderful homecomings each year, one in the spring and another in the fall. People came from churches all around in wagons drawn by horses or on horseback. There was preaching for

Homecomings were held both indoors and outdoors at the Dickason Chapel, inside for the services and the music, then on the grounds for the food. Those who have attended say that there was always plenty to eat! This was the site of the original Dickason Chapel built by Jacob and Betsey Dickason's slaves. Funerals of local residents were held here. Currently, there are services held here once a month. Becky Crabtree.

hours, then food for hours, then singing for hours, then more food. There were dozens of wooden tables set up in the churchyard all covered with delicious breads, meats, vegetables, and desserts. Lake especially liked the pies his Aunt Mariah made and his favorite drink was buttermilk. He liked it so cold that it made the glass jar sweat. He played with his cousins and visited with aunts and uncles and friends. Sometimes the men played horseshoes down by the woods.

Other churches had homecomings as well. He visited Ballard and Union and Greenville churches but his favorite was Gap Mills African Methodist Episcopal (AME) Church. Aunt Mariah and Uncle Elijah Dunlap lived there on a farm and when their church held Homecoming, his family had to spend the night with them before returning home. Such a big house full of children: Baby Faye, John, Mary, Cecil, and

Homecoming Refreshment Stand   #44
Dickerson's Chapel
Monroe County   Fernandez

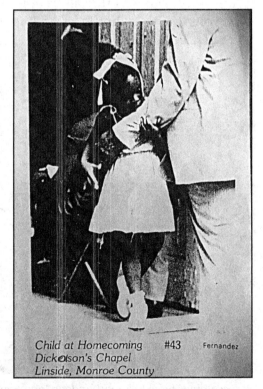

Child at Homecoming   #43   Fernandez
Dickerson's Chapel
Linside, Monroe County

Left: Refreshment Stand at Dickason Chapel near Lindside, WV in early 1960s, Brooks Gore with Mona Walker Dixon. The two are pictured near where the 'Six-Log Church' stood from 1841-1921. Right: Child at Homecoming at Dickason Chapel near Lindside, WV in early 1960s. Black Diamonds, a booklet published by John Henry Memorial Foundation, Princeton WV, about 1960. Photo and identification courtesy of Mary Ross.

Delbert who was born the same month and year as Lake. The boys counted the days between their birthdays and discovered that Lake was eleven days older. This became very important when Lake needed authority to make decisions like what game they would play or what story they would read. The boys didn't see each other often, but when they did, they were inseparable.

The AME Church at Gap Mills located near the Dunlap farm in 2017. It was constructed in 1899, the summer before Henry Lake turned 13. It replaced the log church building that was likely built by slaves. Homecomings here continued into the 1980s. Becky Crabtree.

Mariah and Elijah Dunlap's farmhouse in Gap Mills, WV, in 2017, more than a hundred years after the homecomings of Henry Lake and Delbert's childhood. Becky Crabtree.

Chapter 5 – Winter

During the cold winter of 1894–95, there were few reasons to travel. Even regular church services were canceled because the weather was dangerously cold and there were deep snows. In January, school closed for weeks because the snow was so deep that the students dared not walk to class. Instead, they helped at home. There was wood and water to carry and animals that needed to be fed a little extra.

The Dickason cabin had become a makeshift hospital for Hattie. By then, she was too weak to get out of bed so her parents moved her cot into the front room. It was plenty warm there with both the cooking stove and the fireplace putting out heat.

Lake overheard whispers between his parents while Hattie slept. Momma asked Papa, "How much more can her little body stand? She hasn't eaten a bite since Christmas. You must go get the doctor."

Then bitter replies from Papa, "No need to go to Lindside for a doctor, he couldn't get through the snow and there's no use anyway. Consumption." He choked on the word then went on. "You remember what he said last fall that she wouldn't see Christmas. But she has. Our little girl made it to the New Year, too!" Lake felt his father's pain as he held Fannie tightly to calm her cries of grief. "Shhhh, Momma, don't let it take you away. Hattie still needs you and Lake and I need you, too."

Month	Snow, Ice (inches)	Average Temperature High/Low
December, 1894	42/23 (Westernport, WV)	
January, 1895	16.5 (Union, WV)	34/1 (Westernport, WV)

Weather near the Dickason cabin during the 1894–1895 winter. Record of Climatological Observations, U.S. Department of Commerce, National Oceanic & Atmospheric Administration, National Environmental Satellite, Data, and Information Service.

Lake didn't completely grasp the seriousness of Hattie's illness until he saw the blood on her pillow. Whenever she coughed, she spit up blood. And she was too frail to even cover her mouth with a handkerchief or towel so she coughed into the pillows, more blood than her mother could keep cleaned up.

Hattie passed away in the early morning hours of February 6, 1895. Somehow Lake thought she would at least be there for her birthday in April. She had talked of being ten years old and he thought that not making it was almost as unfair as her death.

Grandpa built the child-sized wooden coffin and they took her body to the Dickason Chapel for services. Mercifully, her burial took place between snowstorms, but the frozen rock-hard earth had made the digging of her grave agonizingly slow. There was too much snow on the ground for the wagon to get to the graveyard so her uncles had to carry the coffin, stumbling up the last steep steps. Guy held Fannie as they followed the procession and Lake trailed behind with his cousins. The graveside service was brief, a Scripture reading and the lowering of her small casket. Lake would always remember his horror at the sound of a shovelful of frozen soil hitting the boards of her wooden casket.

The Dickason cabin was a sad place the rest of the winter. It was as if her passing cut the strings that held the family together. Each member of the household spent most of their time alone, Lake reading or working, Momma cleaning everything, sometimes twice, and Papa spent much time in the barn in the evenings. Lake tried to help each of his parents the best he could but sometimes the sadness settled into his chest and ached and ached.

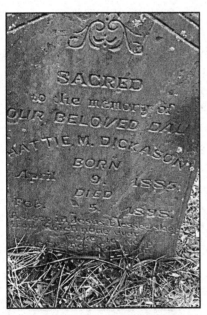

Hattie Dickason's (1885-1895) final resting place in the Dickason Family Cemetery. She was Henry Lake Dickason's sister and died as a child. Becky Crabtree

Chapter 6 – Spring

When the weather finally broke in mid-March, 1895, the road turned to mud. By then so many school days had been missed that students could not take the examination to move up a grade. Plowing and planting began for the next growing season. Every student had another job now, that of farm laborer. Lake was no different. As an only child, Lake tried to help his momma in the kitchen and his papa in the barn and the fields and was working long hours day in and day out. It was as if they all three were fighting the pain of missing Hattie by tiring themselves so they immediately went to sleep when night came. There were few conversations and fewer tender embraces. The only day they didn't work from daylight to dusk was Sunday.

One chilly Sunday afternoon, Lake had been walking in the woods with Sampson, his foxhound, when the dog bolted for home, yapping his head off down the lane then bawling like he had smelled a fox. Lake ran to see what could be causing the racket and met two horses pulling a wagon load of people. They had company! Aunt Mariah and Uncle Elijah Dunlap and some of their children piled off the wagon with food and hand-me-downs and late Christmas gifts. It was as if the black and white world suddenly had color again with laughter and shouting and bright quilts filling the yard as they threw off their wraps and jumped down. They hugged Fannie and Guy and Lake over and over. Cousin Delbert, the cousin closest in age to Lake, brought a book to share. Lake had never been so happy to see anyone in his life.

Cecil, the oldest Dunlap cousin, was cautioned to keep an eye on Bertha and Delbert and Johnny and not let anyone play in the icy creek water. The adults went inside while the children swarmed over the front yard. Delbert and Lake immediately paired up and climbed up on a tree stump to look at Delbert's book.

After a while, Guy and Elijah came out on the porch. "Wonder how we could get a message to Grandpa and Grandma to come to Sunday dinner?" Guy stroked his beard and asked loudly, looking around the yard.

"I just don't know," Elijah replied, "I don't feel like going that far, might get sun-kissed since as that ole sun is getting so bright." Lake and Delbert looked at each other. Lake's eyebrows went up as if to question Delbert, who nodded his head three times fast.

"Pa! Pa! Delbert and I will go. I know the way." The boys tore from the tree stump where they were playing to run up the steps of the cabin leaving mud on every step. Out of breath, Lake stopped in front of the two men, chest thrown out like a soldier at attention, "Yes, sir, we can do it." Delbert, a head shorter, stood nodding by his side.

Elijah hid a smile and Guy pretended to think about it. "How old are you gentlemen?"

"Oh, Pa, you know I'm going on nine." Lake didn't understand why his dad had asked his age or acted like he might not know the way to Grandpa's, he'd walked there together with his papa all his life, more times than he could count. Grown-ups were peculiar sometimes.

Delbert couldn't be quiet another second. "Me, too, Uncle Guy, I'm going on nine, too." He was fairly jumping up and down. "We can do it."

"I reckon you two could find your way." Then his voice grew more serious. "Go straight through the woods until you come to the field below the Low Gap then down the trail to your grandpa's house." No straying . . . or throwing rocks. Oh, and better wipe those boots good before you go inside or your grandma will have your hides. Tell them we aim to eat early, by four o'clock so's these folks can head back home before dark. And hurry back."

Lake and Delbert raced down the steps, Sampson loping along behind them as they passed through the yard whooping and leaping.

"Should be back in about ten minutes at that pace," Elijah's voice was full of fun as he pulled a watch out of his Sunday pants pocket. "It's just after one o'clock, we might have time to join the ladies and maybe find a hot biscuit to tide us over before the boys return.

Guy watched the place where the boys disappeared into the woods. "Mighty grateful that you and Mariah came. We've been having a hard time around here. With Hattie gone, it makes Lake that much more precious. All we do is work. Hard work. Him, too. Fannie doesn't have anything much to say to him or to me." He looked at his brother-in-law.

"Give her time, Guy. Nothing ever happened worse than burying your own child. Nothing." They remained quiet for a bit, then Elijah continued. "We have three little baby graves at the cemetery down home." The porch remained so silent that songbirds began to sing and a pair of cardinals, bright male and dull reddish-brown female swooped through the air and danced on a bare tree limb in the yard.

The front door swung open interrupting the birds, "Guy. Elijah. I thought you might be out here. Come on in and sample this buttermilk Mariah brought. I wish our milk churned up as thick and delicious. I need to find out her secret. Come on, now."

The men went into the cabin and pulled up chairs to the table and visited some more about planting and deer hunting and about how there were no jobs to speak of. Every now and then they heard a giggle from their wives in the kitchen and when Fannie came out to bring buttermilk and corn bread to snack on, there were shades of pink in her thin, pale cheeks. Guy felt like his world had shed the drabness of winter and was starting to have traces of color as well.

Chapter 7 – Onward

Life got better after the Dunlaps visited. Lake's mom was happier, partly because she knew a secret. Her sister Mariah had whispered in the kitchen that she was going to have a baby and Fannie was overjoyed for her. Lake and Delbert figured how to get messages to one another by penny postcards in the U.S. Mail. They just had to figure out how to get a penny every now and then and that wasn't going to be easy. Guy was starting to enjoy working again instead of working to forget his sadness. They still missed Hattie and put flowers on her grave up at the Dickason Cemetery, especially her momma, but the ache in Lake's chest had faded.

His momma was still lonesome and sometimes memories helped and sometimes they made it worse. Grandma Nancy had taken to her bed and had been cared for in turns by her daughters and daughters-in-law until her death in 1888. Lake had just been a baby when she died and he didn't even remember her, but she had been Fannie's companion for years. They had walked up to the graveyard together often in long ago years. Now Fannie's evening hikes up the steep hill to the cemetery were filled with the stories her mother-in-law had told her so long ago. Nancy had shared stories about the old folks while they tidied up the graves. Fieldstones marked most of the graves because there wasn't money enough to buy engraved headstones for everyone, but Grandma Nancy had known everybody buried in that field, slaves and slave owners both, and exactly where they lay. In her older years, Nancy had repeated the stories so often that Fannie still remembered every word, but she hadn't thought about them much until she started visiting Hattie's grave.

"I knew Master Jacob's boy Samuel that got shot right over there on the mountain when he was hunting. Samuel's was the first grave dug up here. He died when he was fourteen years old and it 'bout killed his mother, too. She never did have another child." Nancy would rest on a log while Fannie arranged flowers and brushed leaves off the stones. Nancy had gone on and on about the people buried there.

"I remember when they led Master Samuel's horse home carrying his limp body cross ways over the saddle and it was too late. Nothing could be done. The boy was dead." She would pause right there, out of respect every time, and would then go another direction with her story. "Samuel Augustus Pack was my Massa' back then, if a person can really belong to another. In those days people thought they did."

"Massa' Samuel left me in his will to his daughter Miss Betsey so I came here. Right here." She'd point down to her farmhouse.

They didn't know what to buy or where to sell or how to farm, but Raeburn taught them some and I taught them some and they watched and learned and did right fine, I guess. Raeburn built wagons for them and they took tobacco clear to Lynchburg to sell at the market. Long trip. It took two weeks."

Now alone, Fannie's shoulders were shaking as she bent over Hattie's grave. She thought she could hear the little girl's laughter and her voice trying to comfort her, "Don't worry, Momma. I'm all right."

Fannie crumpled to the ground on Hattie's grave with a handful of wildflowers. The tears streamed down her face. She placed the flowers near the headstone and hugged herself as she wept.

After a while, she wiped her eyes and patted the ground above

---

1st I give to my former Slave James Dickason (Colored) the tract of land where he now lives ...

2nd I give and bequeath to my former Slave Lewis Dickason (Colored) Seventy two acres of land where he now lives ...

3rd I give an bequeath to my former Slave Hugh Dickason, col'd, son of Reaburn the tract of land I recently bought ...

4th I give to Fanny Dickason Daughter of Reaburn One Milch Cows ...

5th The residue of my property both real and personal I give and bequeath to my former Slave Reaburn Dickason (Col'd) ...

6th I hereby constitute and appoint said Reaburn Dickason (Colored) Executor of this my last will and testament ...

Excerpt from Jacob Dickason will dated June 22, 1875. Monroe Co. Wills, Book 11, page 537.

her daughter and got up to visit her mother-in-law's grave. They'd buried Hattie at the head of her Grandma Nancy's grave. Raeburn had bought, in turn, a tall headstone for each of them, engraved with names and dates of his granddaughter's and his wife's birth and death. He told the stonemason over at Hinton on both occasions to "engrave it deep enough to last a hundred years."

Fannie cleared her head and trudged back down to the big frame house where Raeburn lived alone to check on him before she headed back to the cabin.

Nancy Jane Pack Dickason (1822-1888) was buried in the Dickason Family Cemetery. She came to the farm as a slave, an inheritance to Elizabeth (Betsey) Dickason at the death of her father, Samuel Augustus Pack. Nancy became the wife of Raeburn Hall Dickason Dr. Henry Lake Dickason was their grandson. Becky Crabtree.

Chapter 8 – Bernie

Lake continued his elementary school studies for several more years. He loved reading and read everything that he could find. His math was not as good but he knew farming math: how much seeds cost and how much to buy and what the selling price must be and how to measure to build a wagon. He was nearing the end of his elementary education in 1899 (far beyond the stories of the third reader) at twelve years old. His mother had been feeling poorly and he was worried about her, but his farm duties had grown to nearly a full-time job and he thought of little else.

Then, on a bright May morning in the midst of planting, Aunt Mariah arrived in a rush with Delbert and Baby Bill. Uncle Elijah wasn't with them and a strange man was driving. Lake hurried from an upper field to greet them.

"Your Uncle Elijah couldn't get away right now." She was short when Lake asked about him. "Delbert, you and Lake get those grips out of the wagon and unload those baskets of food and take them inside. Don't wake William. We'll let him sleep for a bit."

"Yes, ma'am." He wanted to ask where Cecil and Bertha and John were but shook his head instead. Strange doings.

Guy came to the door, "Your mother is busy so you and Delbert take care of Baby Bill." He was not his usual relaxed self. "Go, get the baby and go." His voice was loud.

"Yes sir." Lake put down his load on the porch. He had grown so much that he had to turn his feet sideways to get down the steps, but he hurried and went back to the wagon with Delbert and the baby, who, until then, was still fast asleep. The noise awakened the infant and he opened his eyes screaming.

Lake was flustered at the unusual tone of Guy's voice combined with Baby Bill's screaming. Worry for his mother began to grow.

Then there was another sound, his mother's shriek. An ominous silence followed before Baby Bill got his breath again and starting wailing and wiggling in Delbert's arms. Lake watched his father collapse in a rocking chair on the porch. After several minutes that seemed much longer, Aunt Mariah came to the cabin door, "Come on in, Guy. Fannie wants you. Guy stumbled through the half-open door, grabbing both the facing and the doorknob to get through.

"Delbert, give me that baby before he wakes the dead." Mariah took the infant and he smiled through his angry tears of a few seconds before.

All Lake could do was watch the events as they unfolded. He turned his head to watch Delbert shrug at him, at Aunt Mariah getting the baby settled, at the closed door, and to the empty rocking chair still rocking.

Then the door was opening and his papa was coming out with a bundle wrapped in blankets, grinning from ear to ear. "Lake, come and meet your brother, Bernie." Lake felt such relief that he laughed at the tiny mouth and nose and fingers and had trouble believing his new brother was real.

The cabin came alive with a new baby. Diapers to wash, a baby to feed; the work never ended, but Fannie and Guy were delighted and so was Lake.

Chapter 9 – Dreams

The country was in a depression; few local jobs existed. Farmers were poor but they had plenty to eat. Some relatives were leaving to get jobs in far off places in mines or on the railroad.

Lake had dreams of leaving the mountain, too, but he couldn't imagine leaving Bernie. The toddler was slender and small with such a sweet personality that Lake spent every moment he could with him. Some evenings he rocked Bernie to sleep on the front porch and remembered that perfect evening eight years ago just before he first started school. The strongest part of the memory was the peace of Peters Mountain and the anticipation of starting school back then. The mountain was still at peace, even when it roared, but Lake's appetite for more education was starting to build, just like it did when he was six. However, now it wasn't going to be as simple as walking down the lane to school. Children of color weren't allowed to go to school with white children. Only black children attended Chestnut Grove School and there was no high school in Monroe County that they could attend. When most of his cousins and friends were finished with little Chestnut Grove School, their schooling was over. Lake wanted more.

There was a school, Bluefield Colored Institute, that opened in 1896. In fact, William Ross, Cousin Abbie's husband, had been the first student to enroll. Lake had heard Mr. Ross talking to his father and grandfather about BCI. Lake would have to get a ride to Glen Lyn, Virginia and ride the train to Bluefield and work when he wasn't in class to have enough money for books and food and train tickets to come home. He thought and thought about it, but didn't see a way.

One evening in the spring of 1903, his grandfather and father and mother all asked him to come out to the porch to talk. Guy started the conversation, "Henry Lake, do you know all you want to know about book-learning."

Lake looked all around him. "No, sir."

"The truth is, son, we need you at home to help on the farm, but . . ." He paused for a few seconds, and then continued. "We don't want to delay your formal education any longer than need be." Lake's father spoke slowly and Lake knew his words were carefully chosen. "We don't have much money but all of us want you to go." Then it was quiet.

Grandpa Raeburn broke the silence. "Shedrick says we can share one of his hired hands if we feed him supper." He slapped his leg and Lake knew he was happy. "And if you go, that'll free up more than one plate of food a day." They all grinned. Lake just nodded but his heart was bursting with excitement and love for his family.

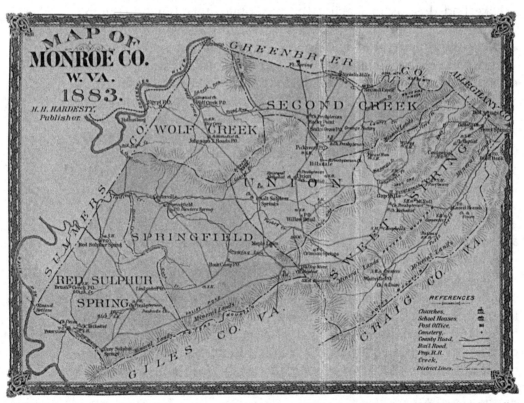

Monroe County, West Virginia map from H. H. Hardesty, Historical & Geographical Encyclopedia which shows Post Offices, creeks, roads, schools, mountains, and timber in 1883. Henry Lake Dickason's home would have been located on the "Valley Road" near the base of Peters Mountain, a road that no longer exists. A copy of this map was published on a 2011 calendar.
"A Glimpse Into the Past" compiled by Monnie Raines Martin and Nedra Pendleton Shaver, distributed at the Peterstown Public Library.

Chapter 10 – Travel

Everyone was up before daylight on a chilly September morning in 1903 so Guy could drive Lake to Glen Lyn, Virginia to board the Virginian Railway train bound for Bluefield and high school. It would have been easier to stay on the farm, doing the jobs he had done dozens of times, surrounded by family and comfortable in the routine there. Without the dream of schooling to guide him, he may have never left home.

There was a tear's path shining on Bernie's face as 16-year-old Lake extended his hand to shake. "You be good while I am gone and listen to Momma and Papa." Lake's formality hid his emotion, but seeing the tear caused him to lift his little brother up and hold him so tightly that he could feel the four-year-old's heartbeat.

Momma was all smiles and love pats. She dusted the shoulder of his wool jacket and wiped imaginary specks from his sleeves. "Now, you eat whatever that school serves and take care of your clothes so you look your best every day in class." Lake knew she just needed to touch him. He also knew that she would hide her tears until they were out of sight.

"Time to go." Guy stomped into the kitchen from outside where he'd harnessed the horses and hitched them to the wagon. He eyed Fannie, "I'll be back just after lunch." Then he nodded at Bernie, "Help your momma, Bernie, and do as you're told. Bernie's lower lip was sticking out, dangerously close to quivering. "Oh, and gather up some apples this morning for Sadie and George. They'll deserve them when we get back."

"Make us proud, Lake." Fannie reached for one last hug and then Bernie had to have another, too. She took the youngster into her arms and followed to the front porch as Guy and Lake climbed up on the wagon's wooden bench. She waved a dish towel and little Bernie clenched and unclenched his fingers in a childish "bye-bye' movement. Lake turned to look back at them and wave and his father whispered, "Don't prolong it. Just makes it harder on her." Lake looked back for another second to memorize the moment, swallowed hard, and then faced the dirt road leading away from all he knew.

"Get up, Sadie. Come on, George." Guy cracked the reins and the pair of horses picked up speed. Lake knew that the view of home would disappear when they rounded the first curve so he closed his eyes then to remember his last view, to press it into his memories.

They rode a long way in silence. It was cool in the morning mists on Little Mountain, but the air was warmer when they reached the west end of Valley Road and turned at Grey Sulphur Springs to go to Peterstown.

They spoke about unimportant things along the way. Guy grumbled about the lack of a closer train station at Rich Creek for passengers heading west. They saw that one farmer hadn't done a second cutting of hay that summer. Another field was full of well-rounded cows. A dog chased the wagon, barking and nipping at the wheels, more for entertainment than anything else.

Finally, as they neared Peterstown, Guy sighed and spoke, "There are sacrifices for greatness." He looked at Lake who was nodding. "Not just yours. Your grandpa insisted that you go, but he will have to let go of working parts of the farm because he can't do it all without you unless the hired hand works as hard as you, which I doubt. Do you have the money for books and for your room and board and for the school fees? Lake reached down and found the precious leather clip purse deep in his pocket and felt the weight of the money there. Any coins he had before this day had been knotted in a handkerchief so he wouldn't lose them.

"Yes, sir, I have it." Guy nodded and they rode on. Businesses were opening in town and there were people on the street. They crossed the bridge over Rich Creek and headed downhill to the village. The horses' job was easier going downhill and they tossed their big heads and manes a bit.

Then they turned right and went up the mountain and around the cliffs until they could see New River and Glen Lyn down below. It was all Guy could do to hold Sadie and George back as they descended again. When the wagon pulled in beside the train station, Lake felt the ache of loss starting in his chest. He hung his head and thought angrily, *"What am I doing, leaving all that I love? My family needs me. I need them."*

His dad clapped him on the back. "Education is your key to the future, son. It gives you choices." Lake looked up, tears blurring his vision. "If you don't go, nothing will change. Yes, we need you on the farm, but we need changes worse. Change takes risks. We are surely not gamblers." He chuckled. "Far from it, but we are willing to take a chance on you. You are a sure thing, Lake."

"Now, sit up straight and try to remember all you know and use it at Bluefield Institute. You are gettin' the opportunity all of us have worked for, especially your grandpa. Dress as well as you can and speak properly and remember everybody isn't like home folks. And Lake, try and be somebody."

Lake responded by sitting up tall on the wagon seat and looking back into his papa's eyes. "Yes sir, Papa. Please tell Grandpa and Momma thank you for me." He breathed out hard and refused to cry. Dignity was all he had left. They hugged there on the seat and Guy thumped Lake's back.

The boy climbed down and removed his leather bag and the pillowcase full of food from the back of the wagon. He watched his dad jiggle the reins and cluck to the horses and turn to head back up the hill. Lake never knew that Guy took the horses down to the river to water them, lit a pipe, and waited and watched until the train came in a streak of black smoke and left, then trotted back by the station to see if Lake had boarded. He was sure he had, but he had promised Fannie to check. Guy grinned and headed home.

Meanwhile, Lake's face was pressed against the train window of the passenger car designated for colored people, looking at the fall scenes before him. The train was nearing Kellysville, West Virginia and Lake was fascinated watching the farms fly by. He remembered that the Monroe Messenger had printed this fact: *A 100-car coal train of the Virginian Railway at Glen Lyn, Virginia, is in two counties of two states crossing two bridges over two rivers, and crossing another railroad twice, all at the same time.* He remembered his uncles and grandpa mapping it out on an old paper poke with much spirited discussion. Lake chuckled to himself as the train wound around that exact length of track.

New River was visible for the first few minutes then the view turned to mountains and cliffs. The train was enveloped in

First student at Bluefield Colored Institute in 1896. William Ross married Henry Lake's cousin, Abigail Dickason and was a Rough Rider with Teddy Roosevelt in the Spanish American War. He is buried in the Dickason Family Cemetery. Bluefield State College Archives.

darkness as it roared through Hale's Gap and then Hale's Tunnel. He blinked at the light when the train emerged then stared at the views from high trestles and mountain ridges. He was in Bluefield before the novelty wore off.

When he got his bag and stepped down from the train and looked around, the driver of a wagon filled with crates from the train waved at him, "Going to the Institute?"

"Yes," was all Lake could get out, testing both his voice and his weak legs alone in a new world.

"Get in, I'm heading that way." Lake climbed up, wondered briefly what was happening on the farm at that moment, and got settled on the seat. They arrived at the school within a half hour and the stranger stopped for him to get off and pointed high on the hill. "Yonder's the school. Good luck to ya, kid."

Lake stood staring at the steep campus, the big trees. He vaguely heard trains coupling in the background and tasted the grit of coal dust in the air. His body relaxed. It felt right. He allowed himself to become excited and trudged up the vertical cement stairs through the terraced hills to follow the destiny his family envisioned.

Though his family knew he would do well, not one of them suspected Lake would become the strong, compassionate man who would eventually change education for both black and white students in southern West Virginia.

Part II

1903 – 1919

Chapter 11 – Bluefield Colored Institute

Lake was assigned a room in West Hall at Bluefield Colored Institute. The dorm boasted steam heat and electricity, both new to him, but the outdoor bathroom facilities were familiar. Constant noise from the train yard just outside his window took some getting used to. Brakes squeaking, cars crashing, and engines releasing noisy steam woke him up at night and startled him during daytime hours. It also took a while to get adjusted to the lights shining outdoors at night; the lit-up noisy world was different from his family's mountain farm. The air was even different; there were whiffs of smoke and coal dust in every breath because the school was so near the train yard of loaded coal cars.

He needed fifty cents a week for his board and room. Bed linens were provided. He had to buy six table napkins as required for entering students. Registration was $5 per school term plus $28.50 for the semester's fees but that didn't include books. Lake knew that he needed a job quickly because his leather purse held only two quarters by the time classes started. He heard older students in the dorm talking about jobs during the first week.

"They're hiring waiters and dishwashers at the Bluefield Inn," a voice came from the center of a group of young men in the hallway. Lake thought about cousin Delbert and his brothers who worked at the Sweet Springs Resort in Monroe County, serving food to the guests and cleaning up after them. He didn't think he could stand around anticipating the needs of the wealthy visitors.

"You ever work there?" another boy asked.

"No, but it's a long walk from school if you can't get a ride and your shirt has to be ironed."

Another boy jumped into the conversation, "You don't want to work there! I got fired because I forgot my tie last year. My mother would've killed me." He grinned. "I didn't tell her, I got hired at the kitchen in the Bluefield Sanatorium and never told her why I changed jobs. At least I had a uniform without a tie!"

Lake joined the group, listened carefully, and thought about his qualifications before he spoke. "Where could I get a job? All I've ever worked is on the farm," he added humbly.

"Shoot, if you want a laborer job, you should go to the railroad or down in the Patch to the mines." The tallest of the young men seemed to know about prime adult jobs.

"No, not a regular job, just a job so I can go to school. I don't mind working hard." Lake was embarrassed by the silence that followed.

"I'm Thad Warren," and the speaker shook hands with Lake.

"Good morning, I'm Henry Lake Dickason." He added, "First year here."

Thad looked him over, "I'd say you're big enough. If you don't mind hard work, and I mean HARD work, you should stop down by Bluefield Hardware. They don't keep help very long."

"Why's that?" Now Lake was really interested.

"The boss man, Mr. Ruff, doesn't put up with any foolishness. He started out as a clerk himself and he knows all the ways to get out of work. If you work for him, you really work!" Thad put his hands on his hips with an air of confidence.

Another boy spoke up, "And the things they sell at Bluefield Hardware are all heavy, railroad equipment and machines and tools for the mines. I heard it was hard work. I have a friend, Hubert, he graduated last year and he worked there 'til he found something else. He had trouble getting up for early classes while he worked there. He was tuckered out every night."

"Thanks, gentlemen." Lake was turning to go back to his room when Thad motioned for him to come with the group.

"Hey, we're heading down to the dining hall, come sit with us tonight, Henry Lake Dickason."

"They call me Lake." He shook hands with all the boys in the group as they introduced themselves and they headed down the stairs, thumping and bumping and laughing like teenaged boys usually travel.

Lake got the job at Bluefield Hardware. He impressed his employer by showing up on time every day and working long hours. Years later, co-workers talked about his feats at Bluefield Hardware. For example, that he lifted 300-pound kegs of railroad spikes three kegs high for hours each day. He got along with his bosses. One of them, Mr. W. L. Thornton, was especially fond of him. Farm work had strengthened his mind and body beyond that of most other young men. The white men and women on the staff noticed his work ethic and quiet demeanor and Mr. Thornton offered him as many hours of work as he could manage.

> . . . Fellows down at the Bluefield Hardware company will tell you that Dr. Henry Dickason, now president of Bluefield State college, is the only man who ever worked in their place who could lift a 300-pound key of railroad spikes three kegs high hour after hour; he worked there while going to Bluefield State; one of his bosses was W. L. Thornton, retired Bluefield Supply executive with whom he has served six years as local draft board executive . . .

This reproduction from the local newspaper reveals Henry Lake Dickason's student work history. Bluefield Daily Telegraph, Feb. 15, 1946, page 5, Craft Memorial Library, Bluefield, WV.

Not only did he work hard at his job, he worked hard in class and excelled as a student. After his initial shyness the first few weeks, he was able to venture his hand up in class to ask and answer questions. Teachers noticed the humble, husky young man who sat in the front row whenever he could, and they engaged him with questions designed to encourage him to think. Lessons in Latin took hours of study and so did mathematics, but reading class wasn't as hard and he enjoyed the thought-provoking discussions. The Bible served as the reading text and Lake was thrilled to be able to write home about new interpretations of verses that he had enjoyed with his family. He wrote long letters to his parents, Grandpa Raeburn, and to Delbert, usually late at night when the silence of the dorm was broken only by young men snoring.

One of his favorite places on the "terraced hills" of BCI was the library, high on the hill above the dorm. Over a thousand volumes were available, most donated from Bluefield citizens who wanted to help the school. He wrote home describing the sunny reading room where a daily newspaper could be found almost every day, "I imagine heaven must be like our glorious library." Although there wasn't much time left in his day between classes, working and studying, he managed to read voraciously in every spare moment.

In his daily life, Lake saw many things at the school and in Bluefield that were new to him. He tried to mentally catalog them to include in his letters. *"Wonder what Grandpa would think of that?"* was a recurring thought. For example, the school had a strict dress code, boys were required to wear a jacket and tie on campus, even for the agricultural classes. Lake stifled a laugh wondering what his grandpa would've thought about him examining fruit trees in a tie. He got used to the strangeness of always being dressed up though, and even bought a new tie when he could afford it, to have a change.

He also got used to the mandatory chapel sessions every Wednesday morning. Students were encouraged to dress in their very best and sit attentively for hours. Guest speakers visited often and there was always a session of moral training during the lengthy assemblies.

Lake was able to work enough to pay his own board and room at the school until graduation in 1906. He had finished high school in three years and was the only graduate of the young school that year. He was eighteen years old.

The wagon bound for the Bluefield train station stood in front of West Hall the morning after graduation. Lake helped load the trunks and other luggage into the back.

"C'mon Lake, sit with me," a girl called and patted the bench beside her. "No, sit with me," called out another female student.

He grinned and put the last bag on the pile, "Guess I'll sit back here with the guys," and a cheer rose up. He grabbed the wagon edge to climb on board.

A deep voice stopped him, "Mr. Dickason." He turned to see Principal Hamilton Hatter eyeing the group who had fallen silent. Principal Hatter nodded at them all. "Students," he

---

Bluefield Colored Institute student life in the early decades of the twentieth century presented a picture of discipline and earnestness.

- Mandatory Wednesday morning chapel services.
- A rigid dress code required jackets and ties for the men and dresses for the young women.
- A draconic honor system to ensure "proper behavior" required permission to leave the campus.

BCI school rules had rigid behavior requirements. Excerpted from Bluefield State College: A Centennial History (1895–1995), C. Stuart McGehee and Frank Wilson.

paused, "enjoy your summer break. And consider returning in the fall. Much depends on you."

He saluted them and Lake shook his hand, and replied in a low voice, "Thank you, sir," before climbing into the rear of the wagon. The departing students, subdued until the wagon left the campus, then began chatting noisily about the school year behind them and the summer ahead.

Lake had been caught up in the excitement of going home but the reality of leaving dozens of friends plus the academic atmosphere in which he thrived hit him with Principal's words.

He sat on his trunk packed with books and clothes, lost in conflicting thoughts as he began the trip home to Lindside to stay and help his family on the farm.

Chapter 12 – Changed

Bluefield Colored Institute had changed Lake's world. At home on the farm, he missed bustling Bluefield. But life on the mountain had changed, too. Lake's younger brother, Bernie, had become a ravenous reader, falling under the same spell of books that had held Lake as a boy. His nose was stuck between the pages of any book that told about foreign lands or heart-stopping adventure at any chance he got. Guy was still teaching at Chestnut Grove School and it had grown considerably. Fannie was thinner but seemed happy. Raeburn didn't go to the fields every day. Instead he spent a great deal of time on the front porch. Lake shook off his ideas of leaving again and went to work. He was warmly welcomed in the fields and at Sunday dinners. His uncles slapped his back and he and Delbert, reunited, talked about current events and education for black students.

At that time, all West Virginia schools were segregated. Lake knew that he had gotten a quality education at Chestnut Grove School and although he was fortunate to have the support and means to leave home to go to high school at such a good school as Bluefield Colored Institute, he recognized that white students could finish high school while living at home. During 1905 and 1906, a black man named Booker T. Washington was raising money to finance Tuskegee Institute, a school for black students in Alabama. It had established a normal school to train black teachers. Mr. Ross, Cousin Abbie's husband, brought over an article from The New York Times and read it after Sunday dinner. It detailed Mr. Washington and Mark Twain at Carnegie

> West Virginia Constitution, Article XII Section 8:
>
> White and colored students shall not be taught in the same schools.

The consitutional requirement that schools be segregated was repealed by West Virginia State Legislature in November 1994. Constitution of West Virginia as Adopted in 1872 with Amendments Since Made, Charleston: Donnally Publishing Company 1905.

Hall in New York City at a fund-raiser. He left the paper as he often did and Lake read it hungrily, over and over.

One warm evening that summer, Fannie fussed around the kitchen after supper and loaded Bernie and Lake up with a bowl of chicken and dumplings, a basket of biscuits and a tin of corn and beans. "Now take that to your Grandpa so he will have at least one good meal today." She peeked under the towel covering the bread. "There's plenty of biscuits there, I think he can have them again for breakfast."

"I think I'll go, Fannie, I feel like a stroll tonight. Will you go with us?" Guy got up slowly from the straight-backed chair at the table.

"Lawd, no, I have things to do around here." She looked at her husband and put a hand on her hip, "Looks like you might feel like a walk, but do your legs feel like one?" Then she waved her dishtowel at him, whipping him gently with it. He grinned and quickly grabbed her for a long embrace that she pretended to fight. Both the boys smiled at their parents' antics, they were used to the carrying-ons at their house. They trudged across the fields with Sampson venturing out with them, old and slow.

"Why do dogs get old?" Bernie questioned his big brother.

"That's the way it is, an earthly body gets tired and old," Lake responded.

"Will Sampson's spirit go to heaven when he dies?" Bernie wasn't satisfied.

Lake wasn't sure how to answer. "I hope so. I figure Sampson will like the streets paved with gold."

"Me, too. Come on, boy." Bernie and Sampson ran on ahead.

"That was the right answer." Guy walked beside Lake. "All he could handle." They walked a ways. "You know he was talking about Grandpa?"

Lake nodded. They were all worried about Raeburn. As they approached the house, they saw Bernie motionless, holding Sampson still beside him. "Shhh," Bernie called, "Grandpa's singing." They all froze in the twilight and listened to his strong bass voice echoing against the mountain from his back porch.

What do we do, Pa?" Lake wondered aloud.

"We go sing with him." Then, Guy hollered, "You got company, Pa" and to his young son, "Bernie, let that dog go." Sampson rambled down to the house and the others followed. Raeburn greeted them from his rocker on the back porch. After fetching a fork and a jar of water while Raeburn cleared a nearby barrel of hand tools to set his supper down, the boys perched on the porch railing. Guy settled in the only other chair. "You still got a fine voice, Pa, when you air it out. Guess we'll entertain you while you eat. Boys, what'll we sing?"

"Steal away, steal away, steal away to Jesus.
Steal away, steal away home.
I ain't got long to stay here
My Lord, He calls me.
He calls me by the thunder.
The trumpet sounds within-a my soul.
I ain't got long to stay here
Green trees are bending.
Po' sinner stand a-trembling.
The trumpet sounds within-a my soul.
I ain't got long to stay here."

"Steal Away" was composed by Wallace Willis, Choctaw freedman in the old Indian Territory, sometime before 1862.

They decided on "The Gospel Train" which had an easy tune and a catchy beat. Bernie added the train sounds that his momma didn't allow in church and they had a good time. Guy let them sing Little Brown Jug that Fannie did not allow anywhere; they all hollered and laughed as Raeburn finished the last dumpling, wiped his mouth and joined in. Lake cleared the barrel and head-motioned for Bernie to join him. They took the dishes inside to wash.

"Son, I am hearing Gabriel's trumpet a little louder these days." Raeburn stared at the beginning colors of sunset spreading across the sky.

"Aw, Pa, maybe your hearing isn't what it used to be." They both chuckled.

"Maybe my mind isn't what it used to be, either." He paused and picked some corn from between his teeth. "Let me tell you what I aim to do next week, while I can." Guy scooted his chair a little closer and leaned forward so as not to miss a word. "I'm going to split the farm up and deed it to all of you boys. The girls already got theirs when they married. And I want Isaiah and Mamie and their passel of young'uns to move in here with me as soon as they can. They'll like that, I think." Guy nodded. "And Mamie can sure cook." Raeburn's dark eyes twinkled just thinking about her cooking.

Lake and Bernie bounded out the open door and headed back to their railing seats. "Now boys, tell your old Grandpa what you aim to do with your life."

"I want more education." Lake didn't hesitate. "Maybe even college someday." He looked at his dad for approval. Guy shrugged. Lake continued, "I want to go back to Bluefield, back to the normal program to teach, but I don't have enough money right now."

Raeburn took out his pipe and lit it. "Every path has puddles, Lake. You'll figure out a way." He turned to look at the seven-year-old. "Bernie?

Bernie squirmed and slid off his seat on the rail, then climbed back on. "I think I want to go to school like Lake and read all day." They chuckled.

"Then what, boy? Be a teacher, like your papa or a farmer like your grandpa?"

Bernie stopped squirming. "I reckon if I could do anything, I'd travel the world and see all the places I read about." No one spoke, but the expression on Raeburn's face was one of approval as he smoked his pipe.

"It's good to have dreams, boy, but it gets down to common sense, sometimes. You got to make it happen, not your folks, not me. You do all you can and leave the rest to God."

They sat and thought about that for a while, then Raeburn continued, "Guy, you still got dreams?"

Guy laughed and said, "Always. Getting these two rascals through all the school they can swallow and then, maybe then," he looked beyond the boys into the darkening trees, "then a house for Fannie with big rooms and a wide front porch, and a furnace."

"That's worthy of her and your life together. Do it, Guy. You choose the land you want from the farm, acreage that sets good for a house. Look it over tomorrow."

He continued, "Boys, we gonna have to work hard and pray to get everything we want done."

Lake murmured, "Vincit diligentia" as if it were a benediction, then told the others, "It means diligence conquers, a BCI class uses it as a motto. I admire it," he admitted.

"Sounds like you learned something at that school," Guy chuckled. "Let's hear another song." So they sang until it was too dark to see. Raeburn loaned them a lantern and the boys chased lightning bugs through the hayfields on the way home.

In the next weeks, Raeburn deeded his farmhouse and several acres to his son, Isaiah. He and his wife, Mamie, and their ten children promptly moved in and cleaned the weather-beaten frame house until it sparkled. He also deeded the remainder of his inheritance from Jacob Dickason to his sons: Shedrick got 61 acres; John Woodson, 70 acres; Guy 78 acres; and Hugh, 2 acres. Hugh had already inherited land from Jacob.

Raeburn lived with Isaiah and family until his death in January 1907. He was buried beside his wife, Lake's grandma, Nancy Jane Pack Dickason, in the family cemetery behind the house. His death was not a surprise. His life had spanned nine decades and his body had slowed down considerably, but his absence left an empty place in the life of every family member, especially that of his two twenty-year-old grandsons: Lake and the old man's namesake Raeburn Sidney.

Sidney, still serious as the little boy who had shared a bench with Lake at Chestnut Grove School, had had to quit studies after finishing that school to help at home. He told Lake after the funeral how badly he wanted to leave the mountain. "Sometimes, I don't think I can carry another bucket of water up the path to the barn or harness a horse once more. I don't mind the work. Truly I don't. But it never changes. Tired of it. Always the same. Every day. And now no more Grandpa to tell me to dream." He covered his face with his hands and cried. It drove home how lucky Lake had been to go to BCI, but he didn't know how to help Sidney.

Lake continued to work hard at home, caring for cattle and planning for springtime planting. He spent a great deal of time with Bernie, reading with him and discussing the happenings in the world always with an eye to his future education. One of their favorite debates was the one Bluefield Colored Institute had planted in Lake's fertile mind: should education be well-rounded, for leaders only, as Mr. W. E. B. Du Bois believed, or should it be mainly industrial, trade school classes so that black students could get jobs, this the philosophy of Mr. Booker T. Washington. Both young Dickasons could argue either side of the highly publicized dispute and they finally dragged their parents into it over supper one night. Guy and Fannie mostly agreed with Mr. Washington's approach because of their love of education but Fannie voiced her opinion as she cleared the table. "Humph. We are Americans aren't we? We work hard as white people, don't we?" Her tone grew bitter. "Harder than some, I expect. Looks like we should be trusted to vote."

"Bernie, we'll leave that fight to your generation." Guy laughingly lit his pipe.

Fannie spoke up, "Move the politics out on the porch if you are going to smoke." Lake was delighted that the issue was being discussed, at his house as well as in the whole country. In the fall, there was a race riot in Atlanta against the accommodationist policies of Booker T. Washington. Black people wanted to vote and be treated equally at work. The killing of ten black men and two white men followed the riot. Du Bois rallied black citizens at the second annual meeting of the "Men of Niagara" held at Harpers Ferry, West Virginia. The world was buzzing with change.

We appeal to the young men and women of this nation, to those whose nostrils are not yet befouled by greed and snobbery and racial narrowness: Stand up for the right, prove yourselves worthy of your heritage and, whether born North or South, dare to treat men as men. Cannot the nation that has absorbed ten-million foreigners into its political life without catastrophe absorb ten-million Negro Americans into that same political life at less cost than their unjust and illegal exclusion will involve?

W.E.B. Du Bois, Niagara Movement, Harper's Ferry, WV, 1906.

One of Lake's friends in Bluefield wrote that summer that Bluefield Colored Institute had a new "Normal School" program to train teachers. Segregated one-room colored schools all over the state had created a demand for black teachers. Lake wrote letters to the school to see what classes he would need and when he heard back, he realized that he could complete the teaching courses in three years. When Lake saw Sidney, he told him about it, and suggested he could go to high school while Lake worked on the higher level, but it wasn't a good time for him to leave. "Someday," was Sidney's close-lipped answer. Lake wrote to Delbert to persuade him to come with him to school in Bluefield but Delbert couldn't. He just didn't have the money, but he vowed to work at the 'Springs' and come the following year. Lake had saved enough to enroll and couldn't wait. He felt that it was time. With the blessings of his mother and father, he packed, hugged Bernie until his heart was bursting, and left again.

Family of Hugh and Laura Dickason, 1907
Hugh Dickason: trustee for Chestnut Grove School, son of
Raeburn and Nancy Dickason.
Seated: Hugh, Laura holding Leonard, Andrew,
Standing: Gene, Lula, and Sidney.

Henry Lake's Uncle Hugh and Aunt Laura with children Hughgene, Raburn Sidney, Leonard, and Andrew. A Glimpse into Lindside Area Schools, Monroe County, West Virginia, Monnie Raines Martin and Nedra Pendleton Shaver.

Chapter 13 – Return

Memories are sometimes different than reality. Lake was amazed at how small the library reading room seemed when he returned to BCI. His memories also did not prepare him for the crowded dorms and the jam-packed classrooms. In contrast, his mental images of Bluefield were smaller than the reality of 1907; the town was thriving. People lined the streets, businesses flourished, and people poured into town from the McDowell County coalfields.

The first thing he did was look for work. Jobs were plentiful, but he decided to stop by Bluefield Hardware first thing to see if there were any job openings. He went around to the back, hat in hand, and stuck his head in the door. "Anybody here?" he called quietly.

"What do you want?" a raspy voice called from the narrow space in the warehouse, followed by cigarette smoke just before a familiar figure appeared into the sunlight.

"Is that you, Mr. Thornton?" Lake whispered, then recovered from his surprise and added in a stronger voice, "Looking for work, sir."

Thornton looked up and down at Lake and broke into a smile, "Lord have mercy, it is Henry Lake, back from the farm. How in the world are you, boy? Hope you're looking for work; we could always use you around here."

Lake bobbed his head up and down, and felt himself reverting to the young man he once was, saying nothing and agreeing with everything his white bosses said, mostly in fear of losing a job. "I'm fine, sir." He raised his eyes to look at Mr. Thornton's face, not quite his eyes, but at least his mouth, and watched him pull on his homemade cigarette. "I'm back in classes at BCI and would like to work here, if you want me."

Earliest known photo of Henry Lake Dickason, probably as a student at Bluefield Colored Institute. Bluefield State College Archives.

"Until you graduate and go on to finer things," Mr. Thornton watched him, eyes twinkling.

"I 'spect, so sir, I aim to be a teacher." Lake took the etiquette risk of his lifetime and met Mr. Thornton's eyes, recognized the humor and respect there, and smiled himself. They shook hands.

"You get settled up at the Institute and then stop by again in a day or two. I'll get you on the work schedule so you can start next week." Lake nodded, fumbling with his hat. Thornton walked back into the building, then looked over his shoulder, "Good to see you Lake; I wondered how you were doing." He stopped and took another draw from his cigarette before flicking it out the open door. Lake walked on air back to the dorm to unpack.

Chapter 14 – Grace

For some reason, most classes were easier than they had been at the high school level. He was able to use the Latin he had learned to quickly advance through the Latin requirements and he had no trouble with history or science or geography.

Only math gave him trouble. He struggled the first two years then had another teacher his last year, Miss Grace Robinson. All the boys worshiped her in spite of her firm voice and business-like approach to teaching. His cousin Delbert Dunlap had saved enough to join Lake at BCI and he whistled under his breath whenever Miss Robinson's name was mentioned. The two men were very close, but that was the one thing that Delbert did that annoyed Lake.

Miss Robinson was slender and dressed fashionably and Lake could understand the fascination. However, he had a hard time with advanced math and tried to downplay any attention to him in class. Therefore, he was mortified when she passed back his Algebra 3 test with a big red "F" on it and a note in prim red handwriting, *"Please see me after class to discuss this."* He couldn't see what he had done wrong and was trembling when the class ended, taking deep breaths to prepare for whatever was next. She walked towards him and leaned on the desk two seats in front of his facing him.

"Mr. Dickason, what are you doing instead of studying?" she asked, her face showing no emotion.

"I – I – I work in town," he couldn't think of what he did but vaguely remembered studying math, too. "I understand operations." He offered. He felt he needed to explain, "I just don't understand equations."

"Did you even read the textbook? Attempt the sample problems?" She crossed her arms and stared at him expectantly.

Letter written to his Aunt Mariah Dunlap by H. L. Dickason in 1911. See Appendix for the entire letter. This document was shared with The Monroe Watchman, Union, WV, by Ms. Justine Nall, of Union and published June 18, 2015.

"Yes, ma'am. I read it all. I worked every sample problem but I didn't understand why they were worked that way." He was shocked. He had never been accused of not trying in school.

"Take your test up front and show me on the board how you solved numbers one through three."

Lake grabbed his paper, staggered to the blackboard and started copying the problems. He finished and wiped the sweat from his brow, leaving a trail of white chalk dust on his forehead.

"How interesting." Miss Robinson walked from side to side surveying his work. "You solved every problem correctly but not using the textbook's methods." She faced him, hands on hips, genuinely interested. "What was your thinking? How did you learn to solve for a variable in this way?"

He gathered his wits and tried to explain as he remembered learning at the oak table in his grandparents' kitchen. "Grandpa showed me on the farm. When we needed seeds, we'd figure how much acreage to be planted, how many rows and then reverse the order to see how much we could afford to pay per pound of seed. Oh, before that, we'd subtract what seed we had saved from last year and calculate how much seed in a pound. We just flipped what we knew against what we wanted to know." He paused and looked at her. "Not all this dividing and marking out like the Algebra book says."

"Why, Mr. Dickason, let me have your paper back." She seemed sheepish. "Every answer on your test is correct, but your methods were quite unorthodox and I suspected you may have gotten the answers, that is, you didn't solve properly," She was marking out the "F" and writing something new.

When Lake realized that she thought he had cheated, he was partially paralyzed. "I would never do that. Never." He wasn't even sure if he was speaking aloud or just thinking the words. When he began to feel he could move, he shook his head, unbelieving.

"Please accept my apology for this misunderstanding." Miss Robinson patted him on the arm and smiled. "I enjoy your perspective on math and am delighted to be found wrong. Let's talk again sometime." Lake stood speechless for a few seconds then exited down the hallway and stairs and ran all the way to West Hall.

He found himself very disturbed. Angry because he was practically accused of dishonesty, scared because such an offense would have broken the BCI Honor Code and ended his school career, and furious that this tiny teacher had doubted him and then smiled. *Who did she think she was? Just because all the other young men liked her didn't mean he did.* He was resolved to never speak with her again, to get help with math so he could do it the way she taught it and never call attention to himself again.

It was not to work out that way.

The prescribed system of mathematics continued to be a tangled knot of ideas to Lake and as hard as he worked, he couldn't get it unraveled. Miss Robinson remained professionally aloof and he began to ask questions in class and then stay after class for help. Eventually, she taught him the system shown in the textbook. By then, he was smitten. He adored her. Her voice, the way she styled her hair, the way her long straight skirts outlined her legs, and most of all, the way she talked to him.

They spent many hours talking. Grace had graduated from Oberlin College in Ohio and had two years of teaching experience prior to coming to Bluefield, one at the Colored High School in Baltimore and one in Summer High School in St. Louis, Missouri. She was three years older than Lake but it didn't cross his mind. He was intrigued that this petite woman had seen so much of the world and had such strong opinions about the role of women and black citizens. Her passion for education rivaled his own and he started considering teaching older students than those he thought he was preparing for, the younger children at one-room rural schools. A city girl, Grace listened with great interest to Lake's stories of farm and family on Peters Mountain but she also took exception to many of his ideas.

Their conversations included events in the world, particularly those involving black leaders. William Du Bois led the Niagara Movement and later established the National Association for the Advancement of Colored People. Du Bois was an outspoken opponent of Booker T. Washington's Atlanta compromise which asked for money from Northern whites for black schools and agreed to not ask for the right to vote for blacks and not to agitate for equal rights. Sometimes Delbert was included, mostly so the couple appeared to be in a group, but they both valued his input and opinions about the issues that affected them all.

Lake and Grace and Delbert shared headlines about both men over a library table. Grace identified more with the views of Du Bois and Lake saw the world more from Washington's perspective. Delbert was more conservative than either Lake or Grace. The issues were new and complicated and they enjoyed their own philosophical wrangling. Newspapers also told of troubled times in Europe but that seemed too far away to affect life in the mountains of West Virginia. Model T Fords were starting to appear, even in Bluefield. It was an exciting time.

At that time, teachers were not allowed to date or even display affection in public, so conversations between Grace and Lake were always chaperoned, in the library or on the grounds and usually with Delbert present. They had not kissed but Lake was sure electricity sparked between them when they touched. He could not tell her that he loved her although he was sure he did. He knew she would have to quit teaching if they married and he had no way to support her. For the first time, his dreams were drifting from the farm and his childhood home. He knew Grace would not be happy living at Lindside without her teaching career.

He passed a note to her in the library just before Christmas break which read: *I want to teach here with you.* She read it and quickly added a sentence, *Then go to college* and slid it across the table. Lake raised his eyebrows and shrugged to communicate an unspoken *Where? How?* Grace grabbed the note back and wrote furiously, *Lincoln U in Penn., The Ohio State U in Columbus, Harris-Stowe in Missouri.* She folded it once and dropped it on his book as she walked by on the way out the door. His head was spinning, but he gathered up his things and followed her to the classroom.

She was waiting at the door smiling. "You need to apply, Mr. Dickason. You can't teach here without a degree."

"Will you go with me?" His question surprised him as much as her.

"Apply," was her only answer and they didn't speak of it again for weeks.

He discussed the possibility of college with his parents during Christmas break. Guy and Fannie, flabbergasted but thrilled, told him of distant relatives in Ohio and promised to write them about housing and a job. Money was always the underlying concern, but Lake had always been willing to work. They decided The Ohio State University was the best choice, but Fannie thought its name was uppity. "Why in the world do they say 'the' for the name of that college? It's the only Ohio State, isn't it? Didn't it used to be Ohio Agricultural College? Somebody used to work there, hmmm, might have been some of my brother's wife's people." Lake explained what Grace had told him, that the Ohio legislature had changed the name and added "The" to distinguish the school from all the other Ohio colleges as the only land grant school. "Humph, still sounds uppity to me." Fannie ended the discussion.

He also told them about Grace. They exchanged glances but asked no questions. Bernie danced around, singing, "Lake's got a girlfriend, Lake's got a girlfriend!" until Fannie threatened the ten-year-old with an early bedtime.

Lake returned to Bluefield determined to at least complete the application for The Ohio State University. He discussed it at length with Delbert who was enthusiastic and also interested in attending Ohio State. A year behind Lake in his studies, Delbert was sure that his cousin could blaze a trail that he could follow.

During his last spring at BCI, Lake and Grace attended a rare social event, a dance, and stood across the room from one another. Lake stared at her while the music played, knowing he didn't dare ask her to dance, and holding his breath as she politely refused other requests. He thought she nodded at him when the band played "Shine on Harvest Moon" and, in his mind, it became their song from that moment on.

Springtime flew by. Lake played baseball for the fledging school and did well academically, still working hard on weekends and evenings to support himself. He even sent a little money home for his family.

In April, Lake was notified that he had been accepted at The Ohio State University. By then, he realized he didn't want to live without Grace and begged her to come with him and go to graduate school. She declined.

He was distraught for a week until Delbert pointed out the obvious, "Ask her to marry you, man." Then he whistled and tried not to laugh. Delbert had always teased Lake for being dumb in spite of being so smart. Lake just nodded, eyebrows lowered in pain.

Finally, days before the end of the term, Lake took Grace's hand and proposed. After a long pause, she accepted, but with several conditions. It must remain their secret; he must finish his Masters Degree before the wedding and she would keep her teaching job to save up for their future. Lake agreed to it all, his spirits soaring, and sealed the promise with a kiss.

Chapter 15 – Ohio

After a summer on the farm, Lake got on the train bound for Columbus and The Ohio State University. He was joining a student population of nearly 3,000, of which only 28 were black. It was his first time to study alongside white students and he didn't know what to expect. All he knew was that he was going to try as hard as he ever had. His father's words from long ago, "Lake, try and be somebody," echoed in his head.

Distant relations, Aunt Alice and Uncle John, whom he had never met, came to the train station in Columbus to get him and dodged a few 'horseless carriages' as their wagon bumped along to the boarding house run by Martha Parker and her husband. Later, his mother's brother, Issac Bailey, visited and showed him around the city.

Classes started the next day and he was taken aback by the amount of studying that was expected. He wrote home

> I am kept quite busy at my studies. We have from twenty-five to fifty pages at every recitation and it is not a matter of having an idea about the lessons but they must be so thoroughly known that often visitors are asked to come to class and the Profs then sometimes call on any of us to explain the first five or ten pages intelligibly to the visitor.

He and Grace wouldn't see each other until Christmas when he would travel to Oberlin to meet her father, seven brothers and two older sisters. Lake's anticipation of seeing Grace overcame any concerns about her family. During the holiday, the couple had time alone to talk and plan and they caught up on BCI news. Latin had been added to Grace's teaching assignment. Lake's cousin Delbert was sailing through his last year of academics there. Bertha, Delbert's sister was now at BCI, too. His cousins sent their love. Delbert sent a Christmas gift from home, too, a wool scarf "for that cold Northern wind."

Grace's mother had died several years earlier, in 1906, and Mr. Robinson was very protective of his youngest daughter. He seemed to like Lake, though, and spent a lot of time asking questions on a variety of subjects. "Don't mind him," Grace whispered, "He's gathering information to think about after we leave. He forgets that I haven't lived here for years." Frank, her younger brother, shared his room with Lake and they got along famously. Lake was reminded of Bernie, so far away. This was his first Christmas away from Monroe County but Grace helped him forget. At the end of the break, the lovebirds reluctantly parted for the new semester.

Current events were more accessible in Columbus than they were in Bluefield. An assault on Booker Washington was widely covered in Ohio's newspapers during Lake's second semester there. NEGRO EDUCATOR ASSAULTED! the headlines seem to shout. Dr. Washington, the president of Tuskegee Institute was mistaken for a "peeper" in a residential area of New York City and was badly beaten by a white resident, Mr. Henry Albert Ulrich. Others on the street joined in, not knowing the identity of the victim, and Dr. Washington was treated for deep cuts at a nearby hospital. President Taft sent a letter of sympathy for the "insane, vicious attack" and promised his support. A case against Ulrich for assault went to court in New York City and Ulrich was found not guilty. Angry claims of racism were published throughout the country.

Lake was concerned and wrote home to his Aunt Mariah in Gap Mills: *It was a great pity that Booker Washington was assaulted the other day for it has almost ruined the race. For the facts are very much different from what most of the papers relate. As the leading Negro of the country what he does affects the mass of Negroes.*

Despite his class load, Lake found work in Columbus, another laborer job a few hours a week, but with a higher rate of pay. It enabled him to pay for room and board without dipping into his savings. He applied for scholarships and found support for tuition. He found more time to take part in activities on campus. It was as if he turned his homesickness and hours missing Grace into the pursuit of education outside the classroom. He attended political debates, and discussed recent happenings with classmates and teachers. He was surprised to be invited to join a black fraternity, Alpha Phi Alpha, and he devoted himself to the organization. In the little free time he had, he enjoyed live music, any kind, but especially the latest, blues and jazz. The music of W. C. Handy, "the Father of the Blues," intrigued him and they met during Handy's early years of performing. They became life-long friends.

Early Seal of The Ohio State University.
Courtesy of The Ohio State University.

On Easter Sunday, 1913, the rain began. Two days later the Olentangy and Scioto Rivers, which met in downtown Columbus, overflowed. According to Bishop Milton Wright, "The flood was second only to Noah's." Over 500 buildings were destroyed and thousands were damaged. The loss of life stood at 467 statewide. The area hardest hit was a working class neighborhood in Columbus where residents climbed trees to escape the rising water. The buildings of The Ohio State University, on high ground, suffered only minor damage. Classes were only canceled for a day due to lack of clean water but students aided in recovery efforts, evacuating homes, cooking meals, and gathering necessities for the homeless. It was several weeks before the university returned to normal.

Graduation went on as scheduled, however, and Lake earned a Bachelor of Arts degree in, of all things, mathematics, in 1913. He was true to Grace's wishes and stayed in Ohio another year to complete the requirements of a Master of Arts Degree in Math and Physics. Even as his studies became more difficult, he found time not only to be active in Alpha, but was elected the national General President of Alpha Phi Alpha. He was a respected leader and traveled to a number of colleges in the northeast to charter new chapters. For example, in May, 1914, the Pi Chapter composed of students from Case School of Applied Science and the Western Reserve University (which became Case Western Reserve University) was chartered by Henry Lake while he was still a student at The Ohio State University.[As of 2017, the chapter still exists, a city-wide organization encompassing four Cleveland universities. It is currently located at Cleveland State University.] He strengthened communication, both internal and external, by starting a fraternity magazine, *The Sphinx,* to share the values of Alpha Phi Alpha. He inspired his brothers with his thoughtful guidance: *Think Alpha Phi Alpha. Talk Alpha Phi Alpha. Promote Alpha Phi Alpha and labor for the broad principles of idealism for which Alpha Phi Alpha was created so that humanity shall look on us as a body worthwhile.*

Lake's duties as General President of Alpha Phi Alpha kept him away from Lindside until mid-summer when he returned to Peters Mountain, in time to say goodbye to Cousin Sidney. Raburn Sidney had found a way off the mountain; he had joined the army. War was getting closer in Europe. He was assigned the 802nd Pioneer Infantry Regiment and was heading to France to build roads. His regiment was made up of black men, not allowed to have guns. Instead the men carried shovels. His regiment made history in another way; soldiers formed a band, a jazz band, which may have introduced early jazz music to French listeners.

On the mountain, Bernie was home after two years at BCI and was raring to get back and graduate, still reading about far-away places. Guy was giving up teaching at Chestnut Grove to devote time to the farm. He and Fannie were saving every penny in hopes of making enough money to get Bernie through school and to finally start building a new house. Lake had accepted a teaching job at BCI and was anxious to get back to Bluefield and Grace. He spent a few weeks in Monroe County, absorbing fresh air and buttermilk, working in the fields, visiting all his relatives, plus keeping up with Alpha Phi Alpha letter writing. If he hadn't been so anxious to be with Grace, it would have been a relaxing change of scenery from city life in Columbus. Finally, in late August, he packed and made the trip to Glen Lyn to get the train to Bluefield and Miss Grace Robinson.

Chapter 16 – Marriage

Lake and Grace were married on August 26, 1914. They moved into teacher housing at the school. Dr. Robert P. Sims was the principal and having been apprised of the marriage beforehand, graciously offered Grace a part-time teaching job as a language instructor two days a week and a substitute as needed. Since the school was booming, he was glad to do so as the school needed teachers. She jumped at the opportunity. Staying home all day had never appealed to her.

Bernie lived at West Hall like his big brother before him. He did well in his classes and was on track to graduate in 1916.

By Thanksgiving, Grace and Lake knew they were expecting a baby and both were delighted. Lake was determined to provide well for his beloved wife and child and worked harder than ever before. He taught mathematics, was an assistant football coach, and led several school organizations. Student population was at an all-time high and the school's first football team won a conference championship.

Their baby boy was born in the summer of 1915 and was named Henry Lake Dickason, Jr. His parents doted upon every movement he made. They were devastated when he did not survive infancy. Little Henry Lake was buried in the Robinson plot of the Westwood Cemetery in Oberlin, Ohio on August 4, 1915. Lake was determined that his son have a headstone and left Ohio after the services with his father-in-law's promise to have one made and installed.

Lake and Grace struggled through their sadness that winter and only began to laugh again with the return of spring. They visited Guy and Fannie at Lindside during Easter break. When they could escape Bernie for an hour they walked hand in hand through the woods, resting as the path became steep.

Grace was amazed at the views. "I cannot imagine a more beautiful place on earth," she whispered, awestruck at the mountains spotted with pastels, the redbud and dogwood trees in bloom. She turned to Lake, "What is the name of this place?"

"Peters Mountain." He swung his arm the length of the mountain range.

"No, Lake, this place." She stomped her foot and pointed to the knoll just below them.

"It doesn't have a name." Then he added playfully, "You can name it. How proper, for the most revered Latin teacher of all of Bluefield to name this beautiful place."

Grace looked at him, enjoying the challenge and the fun, and, after a few seconds, spoke, "Something about the mountains, so 'mont' must to be part of the name. Let me see, above the mountain, below the mountain, I know – between the mountains. Cis." She was excited and turned to pat Lake's chest with both hands. "Cismont. Say it, Lake, say it."

"Cis -mont, Cismont. I think you have captured it." He tenderly brushed back a stray curl tossed out of place by a breeze and lost himself in her sparkling eyes. "As you have captured me, my darling." He bent to kiss her and the future looked brighter than it had in a while.

View from Cismont's front porch in 2016. There was once an orchard and cattle grazing in the fields below the home. Becky Crabtree.

Chapter 17 – Colleagues

Their lives became entwined in the school family of Bluefield Colored Institute. Grace was much loved by her students and had been there long enough to have many former students as friends in Bluefield and the surrounding area. Many of her "girls and boys" were young men and women teachers in Mercer, McDowell, and Tazewell counties and their doors were always open for her to visit them at school or at home. Through them, she kept up with the needs and issues of the new generation of Negro citizens in Southern West Virginia and Southwestern Virginia.

The Dunlap cousins were well represented with Berta, Cecil, and John all completing programs at the Bluefield school. Lake wrote their mother, his Aunt Mariah: *I should suppose it is a source of pleasure for parents when two or three of their children are getting educations which will be of so much benefit to all concerned and who stand in such great esteem as your children do with the school authorities, especially in Bluefield.*

The cousin Delbert followed Lake's path to The Ohio State University and then joined Lake at BCI in 1917, teaching agriculture and science. By then, Lake had moved from the classroom to an administrative position, the school's registrar. Lively discussions were

1918 Bluefield Colored Institute Faculty. Henry Lake Dickason is shown as Assistant Principal (back row, third from left) and Robert P. Sims, Principal (back row, fourth from left) Bluefield State College Archives.

frequent in the small living room of Grace and Lake's faculty apartment. Delbert and Cecil were often included as was Sidney Dickason, who had returned from France and left the military. He had enrolled at BCI to continue his education and entertained them with tales of France and the war. The school prospered, enrollment soaring and funds allowing improvements to school structures and expansion of the campus. The war was coming to an end in Europe: on the eleventh hour of the eleventh day of the eleventh month of 1918, an armistice was signed and the war ended. Bernie had traveled with a classmate to Cleveland after their graduation and set sail with the DC Navigation Company, a shipping and cruise company on the Great Lakes, happy as a clam. All was well in their world.

BLUEFIELD'S FIRST FOOTBALL TEAM, 1914

First Row — Lawrence Buster (C)   Second Row — Prof. A. A. Turner (L.T.)   John A Dunlap, Head Coach   Third Row — Waren Pickett, Pompey Ross,   James K. Leckett, Wallace Washington.   Back Row — James K. Hulley, Courtney B. Wright, Archibald Adams, Otis Walden, Buckhannon Wight, Stanley Turner, (Q.B.) Fannish, Herman Few.

ATHLETIC COMMITTEE — L. L. Wade, Chairman and Bus. Mgr., A. A. Turner, Head Coach,   H. L. Dickason, Assistant Coach and Secretary.

1914 Bluefield Colored Institute Football Team. The Bluefieldian, College newspaper, Bluefield State College Archives

Chapter 18 – Horror

Then, Grace fell ill on Christmas Eve and begged off attending services at their church in Bluefield. Although Lake had wanted to attend, he took off his Sunday suit and tended to her. Her stomach hurt and when the pain became unbearable on Christmas Day, he called the doctor. Treatment was basic: warm compresses on her tender midsection and a liquid diet, but to no avail. Grace died in her own bed on December 27, 1919. The death certificate listed the cause of death as "acute abdominal gangrene due to adhesions."

Lake made another trip north with a coffin to bury his wife. Delbert accompanied him on the long cold train trip holding his sobbing cousin from time to time during the night. The funeral was

Grace E. Robinson Dickason tombstone in Westwood Cemetery, Oberlin, Ohio. Margaret Christian.

held at her family's home on North Main Street in Oberlin, Ohio and she was buried in the same plot as their son, her name added to his headstone.

Lake was silent most of the way home. His world had collapsed.

Chapter 19 – Brokenhearted

Lake and Delbert returned to Lake and Grace's cold apartment, the bed still mussed where she had tossed in pain. Delbert suggested his rooms for the time being and saw Lake to bed. Before collapsing on the couch, Delbert climbed the hill to Principal Sim's office to let him know they were back. Mrs. Sims was there and said that she'd see that the apartment was tidied up immediately.

The men faced the bleak January together. Lake returned to the he work at the school in a few days but he walked slower, spoke more slowly, and often had a faraway look. Delbert and other members of the faculty ran interference in school matters for weeks. In addition to severing from all social events, Lake withdrew from his family.

When spring arrived, Delbert encouraged Lake to visit Monroe County in hopes he'd regain strength on his beloved Peters Mountain. Lake reluctantly agreed.

Guy and Fannie ran down the lane to welcome him with open arms and plenty of tears. Lake looked thin, but his mother was prepared; she'd been cooking for two days. She served him the foods she knew he loved: buttermilk, fried apples, warm biscuits, fried chicken, stewed rabbit, custard, black walnut cake, and rhubarb pie. Guy was by his son's side, walking mountain trails and visiting with extended family. In the evenings, they shared letters. Bernie was coming back to the mountains to teach, leaving the Great Lakes shipping clerk position for a job in Greenbrier County. It had been several years since he'd been home to visit. Mariah's family was well except for Uncle Elijah, who was slowing down.

At breakfast one morning near the end of the visit, Guy asked, "Son, do you feel like a walk first thing this morning?"

"I suppose so," Lake paused to answer, picking at the food on his plate with his fork. "Where are we heading?"

Guy wiped his mouth and pushed back from the table, smiling, "Momma and I have something to show you." Fannie had already hung up her apron and put on her old gardening shoes, anxious to go.

They led him around the mountain on the same path that he and Grace had taken a few years earlier and stopped among the same budding trees. Lake fought back his spinning senses and took a deep breath to hide his emotion.

Fannie spoke first, "Look, Lake, down on the knoll. See the rocks?" She clasped her hands together in excitement.

His father spoke, "The rocks mark the corners of the house we are planning. This is the place we are planning to build." Getting no response from Lake, Guy continued, "It won't take much leveling, the orchard won't be disturbed, and the hayfields to the west will allow us a full view of sunset from the front porch. The mountain behind us will shade the early sun and block that devil wind. Come, Momma, let's walk down there and show Lake the view from the front porch."

Without realizing it, Guy and Fannie were showing Lake the same spot Grace had loved. They were going to build a house there. Lake hung his head, tears dripping from his face, his chest about to burst from the pain. Frozen in place, he thought he could bear no more. When it occurred to him that he couldn't breathe and the familiar thoughts of his own death surfaced, he turned his thoughts to God for help and sunk to the ground on his knees. Within a second of that unspoken prayer, he felt Grace's hand on his, heard her whisper: *Cismont. Say it, Lake, say it.*

Lake wanted to grab Grace and bring her essence back but she was gone. A tendril of her voice trailing behind her memory seemed to say: *Go on, my love, live, LIVE!*

"Cismont," he said it aloud, shut his eyes, taking deep, shuddering, cleansing breaths. When he opened them, he could feel the breeze, smell the rich earth, and hear the birds. He was hungry for the first time since Christmas. He thanked God for allowing him to feel Grace again, to feel alive again.

His parents had descended to the knoll below, chatting about their plans. *How much I owe them,* he thought and resolved to help them find their dream as they had helped him. Grabbing a sturdy tree nearby, he rose, dusted the dead leaves from his pants and made his way downhill through the woods. Laughing with delight, Fannie led him to the invisible front door and bade him look out the kitchen window of her imagination.

Guy confided as they sat in the grass where porch was planned. "We can't start building right away, but we can dream on paper now. There's a James Warren who has a saw mill down the mountain that I want to talk to when we save a little more."

"Call Mr. Warren, Pa. I can send a little money. I'll be getting a raise next term and I can help. It would make me proud to come home to such a grand house." Lake smiled at each parent, sitting on either side of him.

Guy nodded at him and Fannie, glowing with joy, bowed her head and prayed aloud

> *Glory to God! My soul is happy. Thank you Lord Jesus for sparing our lives and allowing us to watch our boys grow up. Be with our Bernie and Lake out in the world; keep them in your hands. And, praise Jesus for the power of dreams. Show the sinners and the backsliders your light, Lord, and be with those who thirst for your love. Deliver us, we pray, from evil, for Thine is the kingdom, the power of morning, the sunset glory, now and forever more. Amen.*

Chapter 20 – Building

Lake went back to Bluefield Colored Institute much renewed. As he had done after the baby's death, he threw himself into the work of the school. There was plenty to be done. Railroad and mining jobs in the area provided paying jobs for black workers who wanted higher education for their children. The school enrollment doubled and tripled. Lake was the school registrar during this time of growth, and by 1923 was promoted to vice-principal of the school.

Now in his 30s, Lake was close enough to his memories as a student and as a young man working on the farm to understand some of the dilemmas students faced. In fact, his strong memories of the years spent away from the school moved him to action. He remembered missing the discussions and ideas while he was on the farm, and of being in the midst of activity at the school. He had empathy for the dozens of graduates who were teaching in one-room schools nestled into the nearby mountains of McDowell, Mercer, Monroe, Raleigh, and Tazewell Counties, leading the cause of rural education alone. To keep them connected to the school, he assisted the young Alumni Association in starting a newsletter, The Blue and Gold. He wrote and performed an Alumni Song and supported the organization by speaking at Alumni gatherings all over the east.

He hadn't been active in church for a while, but renewed his membership in John Stewart Methodist Church in Bluefield and served on a variety of church committees. He also began studying to be a lay-speaker in the church. His faith had suffered with Grace's death and he worked to strengthen his spiritual life.

Dr. D. F. Delbert Dunlap, Chemistry, 1945. Bluefield State College Archives.

Cousin Delbert Dunlap shared living quarters with Lake on campus. Housing was at a premium at the time. Faculty members were living in attics and shabbily built houses as the town and school grew. Delbert commented good-naturedly, "I guess Lake lives here, I hear him come in late at night and leave early every morning." Delbert was still working on his Master's degree at The Ohio State University as he could during the summer, but his full-time job as a professor teaching chemistry and agriculture took most of his time.

The promise to send money home was not forgotten, and Lake's contributions to the construction of Guy and Fannie's home made it a reality. In 1922, James McDowell Warren, a builder who lived down the mountain a ways, was hired to build the home. Guy helped when he could and it was under roof by fall.

A family reunion was held at the new house in early spring of 1923. The smell of sawdust lingered in the huge rooms of the two-story frame house. The bare walls echoed with loud greetings and laughter. Fannie's sister Mariah and husband Elijah came with all the children that still lived nearby. Guy's brothers and their families all attended. Raburn Sidney, out of the military and established as a school principal in Lester, West Virginia arrived with his wife. Bernie had made good on the promise made in a letter and had arrived the night before. At the dinner table, Lake toasted his parents and family, "To Mamma and Papa and the love that they spread among us all." There was applause.

Guy nodded, encouraging him to go on with a surprise they had planned together for Fannie. "And, to this farm, Cismont, the place that they made happen. There's a sign waiting to be installed at the gate." Fannie was pleased and there were murmurs of pleasure that such a fine house would have its own name. Happy applause and cheers preceded the scraping of chairs as adults made their way to help themselves to cake and pies lined up on the sideboard.

After the last vehicle left, Lake was able to visit alone with Bernie. The brothers were rocking on Fannie's new front porch and decided to walk the fence line. Lake was full of questions. "What's it like on board a ship, day after day?" Where's your wife? Where are you teaching? Do you like it? Would you come back to Bluefield with me to teach?

Bernie told him about the sights and smells of the ships he sailed on and the wife who had deserted him, but was interrupted every few sentences by a persistent cough.

"How long have you had that cough?" Lake asked, concerned.

Bernie raised his eyes over the hand covering his mouth and met Lake's. The big man stumbled and grabbed a fence post, for he knew well the sound, the look of tuberculosis. He motioned back towards the house, "Do they know?"

"No, and let's keep it that way. I had to get up in the night and go outside. The coughing spells were bad. But I got through dinner pretty well."

"Bernie, there's treatments now. There are sanatoriums. They might be able to help you."

1922 Bluefield Colored Institute Faculty, Dickason standing on the far right and Delbert Dunlap seated on his left. The original caption lists all BCI staff as follows Nathaniel Wiley, Librarian; Miss Diana' S. Dent, Sewing; Miss Viola Lewis, Model School; Mrs. Mereides Poindexter, Instrumental Music; Prof. R. R. P. Sims, President; Miss May Marshall, Secretary; Prof. Delbert Dunlap, chemistry; Prof. Henry L. Dickason, Mathematics; Prof. James Coleman, History; Miss Elizabeth Miles, Matron; Miss Ruth Dean, Modern Languages; Prof. S. L. Wade, English; Prof. S. L. Rann, English and Athletics; Mrs. Stella J. Sims, Biology; Miss Truxla Warran, Physical Culture; Hamilton Hatter, Manual Training.. Atkins Photo, Bluefield State College Archives.

"They cost money, Lake. Catherine took all my savings. I can't pay." He had another coughing spell.

"Please, Bernie. I'll write the one at Denmar tonight and we'll see what needs to be done. Can you stay here at home?" Bernie nodded, wiping his mouth and folding his handkerchief.

At Lake's urging, Bernie changed his mind and decided to tell his parents about the TB diagnosis and the hope of treatment. Guy had suspected the terrible news from the first cough and had broken the possibility to Fannie even before Bernie could bear to tell them. They begged him to stay with them in the spacious new house and he agreed but only temporarily, just until he could find help. Lake was almost as concerned about his aging parents as he was about Bernie and hired Rose Hale, a distant relative and her husband, Harry, to live in a small house on the farm and help them all.

Lake also made arrangements for Bernie's treatment. It was a sad day at the farm when the time to go arrived. Guy and Fannie choked back tears as they hugged their youngest son and told him goodbye. Lake rode the train with him to the West Virginia Colored Tuberculosis Sanitarium located at Denmar, West Virginia in Pocahontas County. The Dickason brothers toured the facility and saw the long porches for open air sleeping and the outdoor activities offered, but both were almost too saddened by the reality they faced to have much hope.

It didn't raise Lake's expectations when the application required payment for a train ticket in advance for the return trip either as a released patient or a corpse. Bernard French Dickason was admitted on April 29, 1923 and died on July 22 the same year. His body was shipped home and he was buried in the Dickason Family Cemetery, near Hattie, the sister that he never knew. He was 23 years old.

Bernard F. Dickason's (1899-1923) grave in the Dickason Family Cemetery, 23, the younger brother of Henry Lake Dickason. Becky Crabtree.

Chapter 21 – Renaissance

The years following World War I brought a movement of pride in African-American culture. Many black people had moved north to escape unfairness in the south and settled in an area of New York City called Harlem. During this time, they celebrated their culture through music, art, and writing. The sudden burst of interest was called the Harlem Renaissance; its influence spread throughout the world, resulting in more awareness of African Americans and their perspective.

Bluefield Colored Institute, isolated in the mountains of West Virginia, had always promoted pride in race as a school goal. The Institute played a role in Harlem Renaissance as well, that of messenger for the Harlem Renaissance voices. Noted African American artists and musicians visited the Bluefield school to perform for the community. Often, the famous guests also made side trips to elementary schools and small communities in the area served by teachers who were graduates of BCI.

The school offered a class, *The Negro in American History,* during these years, well ahead of most black schools. The class addition was partly influenced by Carter Woodson, the first scholar of African American history, who visited

I would not deny, or for a moment seem to deny, the paramount necessity of teaching the Negro to work, and to work steadily and skillfully; or seem to depreciate in the slightest degree the important part industrial schools must play in the accomplishment of these ends, but I do say, and insist upon it, that it is industrialism drunk with its vision of success, to imagine that its own work can be accomplished without providing for the training of broadly cultured men and women to teach its own teachers, and to teach the teachers of the public schools.

*An excerpt from an essay from **The Negro Problem**, by Booker T. Washington, et al., a collection of essays written in 1903 by leading African Americans.* https://en.wikisource.org/wiki/The_Talented_Tenth.

– 75 –

"How then shall the leaders of a struggling people be trained and the hands of the risen few strengthened? There can be but one answer: The best and most capable of their youth must be schooled in the colleges and universities of the land. We will not quarrel as to just what the university of the Negro should teach or how it should teach it—I willingly admit that each soul and each race-soul needs its own peculiar curriculum. But this is true: A university is a human invention for the transmission of knowledge and culture from generation to generation, through the training of quick minds and pure hearts, and for this work no other human invention will suffice, not even trade and industrial schools."

*An excerpt from an essay from **The Negro Problem**, by Booker T. Washington, et al., a collection of essays written in 1903 by leading African Americans. https://en.wikisource.org/wiki/ The_Talented_Tenth.*

and addressed a graduating class. Another leader of the movement, W. E .B. Du Bois, familiar to all students at BCI as an opponent of Booker T. Washington as far as educational philosophy for Negroes was concerned, addressed the graduating class of 1926.

Chapter 22 – Respect

Another family tragedy hit when Raburn Sidney fell ill in mid-September, 1926, Surgery was performed in the nearby Princeton Hospital, but he died that evening. Lake was the closest family member in neighboring Bluefield other than Raburn's wife, Cleo, in no shape to handle more, so Lake took care of the arrangements for his cousin. Again, Lake and his family made their way up the steep hill to the Dickason Cemetery to bury a loved one.

Lake and his parents stood on the upper side of the cemetery with the vista of mountains and valleys before them, framed by the lush foliage of late summer. The edges of leaves were just beginning to change to reds and yellows. Lake saw the beauty but his eyes kept coming back to the graves of those he had known. Except for his grandmother's, none of them were marked, except with rounded field stones. Hattie and Bernie and Raburn and now Sidney, all without even a name on their final resting place.

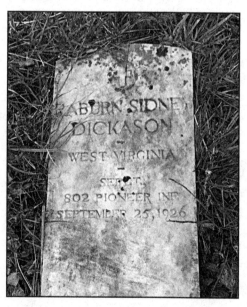

As they walked the lane towards home together, Lake ventured a question. "Why don't we have tombstones for family in the cemetery? Jacob and Betsey and their son, the white folks, have them."

Guy answered, "Your grandpa took care of that over at Hinton, but Jacob paid. Your grandpa saved and bought one for your grandma, but mostly we

Tombstone of the cousin of Henry Lake Dickason, Raburn Sidney Dickason (1895-1926) was the principal of the school at Lester, WV at the time of his death. Becky Crabtree.

SIDNEY DICKASON DIES

The funeral of Sidney Dickason. who underwent an operation at the Princeton Hospital last week, died Saturday evening about 8 o'clock and was buried yesterday at his home at Lindside. Mr. Dickasonis well known in Bluefield where he attended the Bluefield Institute. At the time of his illness he was conducting school at Lester where he had served as principal for several years. Prof. H. L. Dickason,as sistant president of Bluefield In stitute, cousin of the deceased, at tended the funeral and burial.

Sidney Dickason's death and funeral was reported in the local newspaper. Bluefield Daily Telegraph, Sept. 29, 1926, page 11, Craft Memorial Library, Bluefield, WV.

don't have the money to spend. That's the way it's always been, son, not disrespect, just practical matters."

Lake didn't say a word but he vowed to change that family tradition, to find out the cost and mark his brother and sister's and Sidney's grave, at least with their name and dates. It was the least he could do.

Chapter 23 – Flossie

Principal Sims and Mr. Dickason were deep in conversation around the principal's desk, trying to stretch school funds to purchase books and science lab equipment when the secretary tapped with her knuckles on the inner office door. "Dr. Sims, the new teacher is here and wants to meet you."

Sims looked up, "You have the housing information for her, don't you?"

"Yes, sir."

"We completed her contract and it's ready for her to sign, correct."

"Yes, sir."

Sims looked at Lake then at his secretary. "Miss Marshall? Why does she need to see me?"

May Marshall sighed. "I don't know, sir, but she sure intends to meet you. What must I do?"

Lawn view from near Conley Hall. Bluefield State College Archives.

"Show her in, I guess." He placed his pencil on the desk and Lake straightened the papers they were working on.

A tall, shapely woman appeared in the door and paused. Her red hat was tilted over one eye, the attached black veil bunched up on the brim. Her matching red dress had a flared skirt dancing at mid-calf. She clutched a purse to her side with a black-gloved hand. Both men rose to greet her.

She hesitated before speaking a throaty, "Good morning."

"Hello," President Sims answered, and stepped forward. She offered her hand as if it were to be kissed but he grasped it instead and turned it into a handshake.

"I am Flossie Mack, formerly of Milner, Georgia, here to teach," she drawled in the unmistakable formality and accent of the Deep South.

"Welcome, Miss Mack, Mr. Sims, your principal," he swept an arm towards Lake, "and this is Mr. Henry Lake Dickason, your assistant principal." Lake also took her hand.

"A pleasure to make your acquaintance. How can we assist you this morning?" Lake was almost amused at the boldness of this self-possessed young woman.

"I think all is in order, I simply wanted to meet those in charge and get a feel for the school." She looked all around the small office as if cataloging the sparse furnishings, letting her eyes rest

National Champions! BSC Football (1927). The Bluefieldian, Bluefield State College Archives.

on the framed photographs of BCI's undefeated girls basketball team of 1924 and two recent football teams, both national football champions, then she focused on the two men.

May cleared her throat from the doorway just before a sturdy middle-aged woman dressed in a worn brown suit jacket and straight skirt bustled in.

Dr. Sims introduced them, "Ah, Mrs. Sims, good morning. Please make welcome our new teacher, Miss Mack. She hails from Milner, Georgia. Miss Mack, this is my wife, she is the preceptress of our school."

Stella Sims took her hand, "We are glad you are joining us, Miss Mack. I've come to show you to your housing and there are two students standing by to help with your luggage." She addressed the men, "Dr. Sims, Mr. Dickason, excuse us, while I show Miss Mack her lodging." Then she spoke to Flossie, "Later, this afternoon, I can show you the campus."

"Why, thank you, Mrs. Sims." Flossie's voice was light, but her gaze lingered on the men. "Good day, gentlemen."

Sims closed the door chuckling. Lake commented, "That was lucky that Mrs. Sims happened by." Dr. Sims roared with laughter.

"What?" Lake was bewildered.

"Miss Marshall wasted no time in getting Stella here, did she? She thought we needed help, Lake. Do we really run this place or does my secretary?"

Over the next few months, Miss Mack caught Lake's attention often, as she had a number of issues with students and with the adjustment to life in Bluefield. Dr. Sim's handed her complaints over to Lake to solve. At first, he felt she was a nuisance, but as she explained the reasons for her seemingly constant disputes, he was more inclined to agree with her, at least in principle.

Chapter 24 – Guy

Mr. Dickason's secretary, May was out of breath as she raced down the stairs of Connolly Hall to catch up with Lake who was heading home at the end of a warm August workday. He had his suit jacket thrown over his shoulder and his hat in hand when he heard her, "Mr. Dickason, Mr. Dickason. Stop, oh, stop, there's a message for you." He turned to see her scampering down the steep steps, a paper in her hand, and Delbert huffing and puffing behind her to reach them. "Oh, Mr. Dickason, there's been an accident. Your father." Lake froze sideways on the step as she paused and searched the message. "A Dr. Bradley is bringing your father in an ambulance to the Bluefield Hospital. He has been hurt on the farm, cut by a mowing machine. His nurse called. They left about an hour ago." She was partly reading and partly filling in the blanks from her memory. When she finished, she closed her eyes in pain. Delbert joined them, panting, hands on knees.

Lake pushed up both long sleeves of his shirt and looked around the campus below him as he spoke between gritted teeth, "Those blasted horses. I've told him and told him we could get a tractor." His tone changed to one of decision-making, "I'll go borrow Dr. Sim's coupe. Delbert, can you go with me?" Delbert nodded and Lake bounded back up the steps, taking them two at a time with Delbert in his wake.

Lake paced the sidewalk as he waited at the Bluefield Hospital's colored entrance for another hour until the ambulance arrived, lights flashing. Lake looked beyond the bloody mess of sheets surrounding his father's foot and moved quickly to take his father's hand. Guy opened his eyes and smiled weakly as his stretcher was carried into the hospital, Lake by his side.

Fannie was waving Dr. Bradley to leave her, "Go on, go with Guy, Doctor. I don't need any help." He continued to lead her out the back of the ambulance until Delbert relieved him by taking her hand, then he hurried into the hospital. "It's bad cut, Delbert," Fannie explained. "He was standing between the mowing machine and the horses and they jumped and the machine caught his leg near his foot. It's cut bad, to the bone."

"They're taking him to sew it up," Lake repeated what the doctor had told him. "They'll come and get us when they're done."

The Bluefield doctor came out to talk to the family after several hours, "We are not sure we can save Mr. Dickason's foot, but the bleeding has stopped. We're going to admit him to the hospital and keep watch on him for a few days."

"Is he in pain?" Lake was wringing his hat in both hands.

"Very doubtful; he was given Laudanum at the scene and then we sedated him for the surgery."

"Whatever he needs, Doctor, we stand good for it." The doctor nodded and told them they could take turns sitting with him. He was never alone in the hospital. Either Lake or Fannie stayed at his bedside, but blood poisoning set in. While he floated in and out of consciousness, he had some lucid moments. He seemed so clear thinking at times that his wife and son felt he was getting better. Once, he scooted up in the bed and patted Fannie's hand and told her how happy he had been with her, "walking home to a lighted window knowing you were the light shining inside our cabin" and thanking her for "working like a field hand beside me in the hard times." His eyes sparkled talking about Hattie and Lake and Bernie as babies and when he slid back down into delirium, Fannie tucked the sheet around him and stood in the door facing the hallway so the other patients in the colored ward did not see her weep.

His words to Lake were few. "Son," he whispered loudly in the dark silence of the wee hours and brought Lake out of the chair where he was resting. Guy grabbed his arm with surprising strength and shook it a little. "Listen, son. Listen to me. YOU are my son. I am a proud man." Guy struggled to stay conscious but his grip lessened and he started to slur his words, "You, you worked so hard." He fought to keep his eyes open. "You did well. I love you." He swallowed and spoke again, delirious from the infection, "Don't let nobody tell you different." Then, his eyes closed and he went back to sleep before Lake could speak. He died the next evening, five days after the accident.

His obituary was on the front page of the Monroe Watchman on August 8, 1929 and described him: *Uncle Guy, as he was known, was an excellent citizen, honest and upright, and he was held in high regard by the people of both races.*

Lake once again made the arrangements for a funeral and then accompanied his father's remains from Bluefield to the recently rebuilt Dickason Chapel up to the family cemetery for burial. Afterwards, it was more difficult than ever to leave his mother and the farm. He stayed a week longer to take care of his father's business.

Lake was grateful for Rose Hale and her husband Harry, who were able to stay on. He encouraged Rose to spend all the time she could with his mother. Lake turned to his cousin Abbie's husband, William Ross, for advice on managing the live-stock and the crops. Mr. Ross suggested some relatives that might lease the acreage for cattle and care for the orchard and hay fields, so Lake was able to divert some of the load left on Fannie, now 63 years old. She'd see him at Thanksgiving time, he promised.

"UNCLE" GUY DICKASON TAKEN BY DEATH

Guy R. Dickason, an esteemed colored citizen of near Lindside, and a patriach of his race in that section, died of blood poisoning at a hospital in Bluefield last Monday night. His foot was severely cut just above the ankle on the preceding Wednesday when he was standing front of a mowing machine and the horses started suddenly.

After first aid treatment by Dr. Bradley, he was taken to a hospital in Bluefield, but blood poisoning set in and his death followed.

"Uncle" Guy, as he was known was an excellent citizen, honest and upright, and he was held in high regard by the people of both races.

Prof. H. L. Dickason of Bluefield Institute, a son, survives him and a number of more distant relatives.

Monroe Watchman Aug. 8, 1929, page 1, Monroe Watchman archives, Union, WV.

Guy R. Dickason (1856-1929) was Henry Lake's father and lies in the Dickason Family Cemetery beside his wife, Fannie Ross Dickason. Becky Crabtree

Chapter 25 – Attraction

When he returned to Bluefield, he was overwhelmed with paperwork created by the return of students for the fall term. Miss Mack stopped by the office. "Mr. Dickason," she called from the door.

"Come in, come in," he motioned, rose, closed the door, and returned to the mess at his desk.

Flossie approached his desk and stood awkwardly for a moment tracing her finger on his desk, "Condolences for your loss," she ventured. "It must be hard to lose your father."

He put down his pen, pushed back his chair, and sighed. "Thank you, Miss Mack. I do believe you are the first faculty member to extend your sympathy and you are absolutely correct." He tipped his head back and closed his eyes. When he opened them, wiping a tear threatening to squeeze out of one eye, Miss Mack was beside him, her hand on his broad shoulder.

"I care." Flossie's voice was blunt. He had suspected that she did, but he had fought his own growing attachment. Now, the feeling warmed him and he took her hand and pushed on his desktop with his other hand to stand beside her.

"Miss Mack, you've no idea how much that means to me at this moment." He raised her hands to his lips and touched them. Waves of loneliness and grief rolled over him and he wanted to embrace her, but he dared not. She pulled her hands from his grip and placed them palm down on either side of his chest. Their eyes met and she rested her head on his breastbone. His hands found her back and they stood together for several seconds before he spoke.

"Eat dinner with me tonight in the dining hall?"

"I believe so, Mr. Dickason." She pulled back and touched his chest with her pointing finger in a strange gesture of good-bye.

The proprieties of the past had changed quite a bit since he had fallen in love with Grace twenty years ago and so had his position in the school, from student to assistant principal. He threw caution to the wind and began to court Miss Flossie Mack openly. They took meals together, attended concerts, and took day trips for him to speak in a variety of locations, including an Alumni chapter meeting in Keystone and a graded school assembly in Maybeury. He took Flossie to visit Fannie and the farm several times within the next two years. On one of their visits, they took a radio as a birthday gift. Fannie was delighted. In 1932, the couple eloped.

Chapter 26 – Change

"Delbert," Flossie squawked, "get these beds broken down and put one up for storage and one for you to take upstairs."

Delbert mumbled "Flossie-bossie" in protest but not loud enough for her to hear as he packed wooden crates with his books and clothing. The new wife was moving in and Delbert was reassigned to another, smaller apartment. It wasn't the moving he minded as much as the tone of Lake's new wife.

"Hey, Mrs. Dickason," thundered Lake through the door. She ran in her stocking feet to him and reached up for an extended kiss.

"Don't mind me," Delbert covered his eyes with mock modesty and carried a crate heaped with possessions out the door.

The new Mrs. Dickason devoted her energy to entertaining, keeping house, and supporting a wide variety of causes both in Bluefield and back in "Old Monroe" as she called neighboring Monroe County. She enjoyed her heightened status and as soon as a replacement could be found, she quit her job and became a hostess for the school's social events.

She was often proactive about racial unfairness. During their travels, Lake had to lure his wife away from restaurant managers and train station clerks who often felt her wrath concerning the bathrooms and water fountains set apart with signs marked "White Only" and "Colored."

Typical sign seen during the days of segregation in America. Library of Congress Prints and Photographs Division Washington, D.C. LC-USW3- 037939-E.

Chapter 27 – School Happenings

During those years after World War I, Bluefield Colored Institute was as big and busy as it had ever been. Enrollment grew and Dr. Sims and Mr. Dickason were hard-pressed to keep up with all the many needs and plans they had to improve the school.

Mr. Dickason surveyed graduates as to their continuing educational needs. One of the changes suggested was the addition of summer school sessions, making it possible for teachers to continue their education and keep their teaching jobs during the school term.

Athletics flourished. Both men's and women's basketball teams competed in conference. Individual sports of track and field and boxing also competed interscholastically. Baseball and football were perennial strengths against such rivals as Wilberforce University, Howard University, and West Virginia State College. Campus sports included fencing, archery, and gymnastics.

Dr. Sims was adamant that the athletes model exemplary behavior. He directed the development of a set of rules for sports participants, *An Athlete's Code*.

Student organizations sprung up to further academics and arts. The Biology Club, the Home Economics Club, both men's and women's Glee Clubs, and an Aesthetics Club were popular. The YMCA and YWCA were the largest student groups on campus. Social life was not neglected, either. African-American Greek fraternities

An Athlete's Code
We, Bluefield Institute's athletes, believe and practice the following principles in all our games:

1. We accept defeat in the spirit that we lost to a better team and have always a cheer and handshake for our victors. ...

5. We believe that the school and the team is greater than any man or player, so, the best we have is what we give in every minute of every practice and every game.

6. It is our aim to be gentlemen on the field and off the field and we tolerate no cheats, cowards, or muckers in our midst.

Bluefield State College Centennial History (1895-1995) by C. Stuart McGehee and Frank Wilson.

and sororities were chartered. They sponsored community service projects and established life-long affiliations in the community. Mr. Dickason organized the brothers of Alpha Phi Alpha in 1932, the first fraternity on campus. The Alumni Association, long established by this time, provided incredible support to the school. Lake and Delbert were early members of the Mercer County chapter. Football homecomings brought back hundreds of graduates every year for elaborate festivities. Graduates out in the world were putting Bluefield Colored Institute on the map with their accomplishments.

The national Negro pride movement was evident on the school's Bluefield mountainside where performances by musicians including The Hampton Choir, Count Basie, Dizzy Gillespie, and Duke Ellington packed Arter Gymnasium.

BCI's Commercial Department developed a successful Cooperative Store on campus, owned and run by students. Profits were used to support students with scholarships. The structure of the store was complimented in W. E. B. Du Bois' book *Dusk of Dawn: An Autobiography of a Race.*

Instructors at BCI were active in the community. Sims and Dickason both were in demand as speakers for churches, schools, alumni groups, and educational conferences. They also were regulars on local radio broadcasts. Cortez Reece, Chairman of the Music Department led school choirs to perform all over the region. His study of railroad and mining work songs led to a collection of Appalachian music never before recorded. Joseph E. Dodd, art professor, created the seal depicting a coal miner and a school teacher kneeling at the side of Athena, the

REVIEWS BOOKS

Dean H. L. Dickason was the chapel speaker Wednesday morning. Mr. Dickason made the occasion interesting to the students by giving a brief review of the two books whose authors are former students of the institution. "The Negro in American National Politics," by Prof. William F. Nowlin, asssistant principal of No. B. Elkhorn high school, and "A Scrap Book," by Noy J. Dickerson, principal of school at Jenkinjones. Announcement of the authors brought generous applause from the student body. In closing his review, the dean suggested the qualities tht made a worthwhile individual. He must use language precisely and accurately; secure facts before concluding; be a lady or a gentleman; render an unstinted service, and make an effort to live as well as make a living.

"Reviews Books" news item in the December 6, 1931 issue of the Bluefield Daily Telegraph, Bluefield, West Virginia, gives insight into the qualities that Henry Lake Dickason valued. Bluefield Daily Telegraph, Dec. 6, 1931, page 3, Craft Memorial Library, Bluefield, WV.

goddess of wisdom, an appropriate image representing the school's mission.

Bluefield Colored Institute's lofty expectations were sowing seeds of racial pride and strength throughout southern West Virginia and southwestern Virginia with every program and every successful graduate.

In 1931, the school's name was changed to Bluefield State Teachers College and the high school curriculum was dropped. The humble little school had become a college.

School administrators, Dr. Sims and Mr. Dickason, became President Sims and Dean Dickason. No matter what they were called, they had their hands full.

Funding for new facilities and equipment for the school remained a huge obstacle. The needs of the community were ever changing and so were the social and employment status of Black Americans. Leadership in the field of Negro education was a complicated, difficult business.

I am an earnest advocate of manual training and trade teaching for black boys, and for white boys, too. I believe that next to the founding of Negro colleges the most valuable addition to Negro education since the war, has been industrial training for black boys. Nevertheless, I insist that the object of all true education is not to make men carpenters, it is to make carpenters men; there are two means of making the carpenter a man, each equally important: the first is to give the group and community in which he works, liberally trained teachers and leaders to teach him and his family what life means; the second is to give him sufficient intelligence and technical skill to make him an efficient workman; the first object demands the Negro college and college-bred men—not a quantity of such colleges, but a few of excellent quality; not too many college-bred men, but enough to leaven the lump, to inspire the masses, to raise the Talented Tenth to leadership; the second object demands a good system of common schools, well-taught, conveniently located and properly equipped.

*An excerpt from an essay from **The Negro Problem**, by Booker T. Washington, et al., a collection of essays written in 1903 by leading African Americans. https://en.wikisource.org/wiki/The_Talented_Tenth.*

Faculty and students posing for a themed "Dutch Day" at the school. Bluefield State College Centennial History (1895-1995) by C. Stuart McGehee and Frank Wilson.

Chapter 28 – Fannie

Lake and Flossie visited the farm often during those years, mostly for a change of scenery and the stress free hours it provided. Lake had purchased an automobile and they could easily motor to Lindside on a Friday evening and back to Bluefield to work on Sunday evening. Even though Flossie enjoyed life in town, she was quick to learn the way of life on Peters Mountain and contributed her taste in home decor. She selected the finest in linens, china, and silver for the dining room. Lake's collection was one of books; he had shelves built in a downstairs room to create a library in the house.

During one extended visit in the spring of 1933, Fannie was getting around less and less. Lake knew she was a diabetic but she took care of herself and had cut way back on sweets. When Lake asked what was causing her to limp, she told him she had cut her toenails too short and they were sore. He laughed with her, but soon her toes were so tender that she winched in pain to take even a step and spent most of her day seated, alternately chilling and burning up. She was pale but she didn't complain.

One morning, she was late getting to the kitchen for breakfast. When Rose went to check on her, she found her unmoving in the bed and called for Lake. He rushed in and found her barely conscious. He shouted, "Flossie! Rose! Get her dressed and put blankets on her I'll bring the car around." The women put clothes on her and bundled her up. Rose packed an overnight bag and rode in the back seat with her.

"I'll stay back and watch the farm," Flossie volunteered. Lake nodded and gave her instructions about watering cattle and gates that were to be closed, "If you need more than that, Harry will be off the mountain and home for lunch, just tell him what you need." They sped to Providence Hospital in Bluefield. Fannie was admitted and Lake sat with her waiting for a doctor until that evening. The immediate treatment was to amputate one badly diseased toe. She was in and out of the hospital for several weeks until the infection took her life.

Lake thanked his mother over and over during the last weeks of her life, usually starting the conversation with, "Momma, do you remember . . . ?" Then, he'd finish the question with a time when she did extra for him, like "when I tore my good jacket and I didn't tell you and you stayed up late to sew it so I could wear it the next day? Did I ever thank you for that?" or "when the big boys called me names at school that I didn't understand and you told me I didn't need to understand trashy talk? Just you waving it aside made me quit worrying." He watched her sink lower and lower. His pain and frustration was obvious when she died and he rejected any attempt Flossie made to comfort him.

Her life was remarkable. Fannie Ross Dickason was the daughter of slaves and had married a son of slaves of her own free will at seventeen. She had worked beside her husband for nearly a half century in a mountain cabin. There was neither running water nor electricity but she had learned to read and taught her children to read. She sang as she cooked and fed her family the food she had helped grow. She buried two of three children, lost to a disease for which there was no cure, and a husband whose life could have been saved in another dozen years by antibiotics (as hers could have been). The old folks looked to her for food and support and her sister Mariah adored her. Her sons both survived to adulthood and both earned college degrees against all odds. Lake felt the loss of his mother deep in his chest and could scarcely move on the day of her funeral.

Fannie was buried beside Guy and near Bernie and Hattie in the family cemetery. Her obituary in the Monroe Watchman ended

Fannie Ross Dickason (1866-1933) rests in the Dickason Family Cemetery. In her obituary, she was praised as a follower "of the faith of her profession, a staunch worker and supporter of the church" and for being "a conscientious mother and housewife and the community and state, an honorable and upright servant of the human family." Becky Crabtree.

with: *She leaves a host of immediate relatives and friends to sorrow at her going. In her leave-taking the church has lost a faithful worker, the home a conscientious mother and housewife and the community and state an honorable and upright servant of the human family.* The same issue noted: *Quite a large crowd, both white and colored attended the burial of "Aunt" Fanny Dickason here last Saturday evening.*

School was nearly starting before Lake was himself again, but he was finally able to allow his wife to comfort him and thanked his lucky stars that he had her by his side. He returned to Bluefield ready to work. Rose and Harry stayed on to maintain the farm and ready the house when needed.

Cismont, a lovely home at the base of Peters Mountain in Monroe County, WV. Dreamed of by Henry Lake and Grace Dickason, planned by Guy and Fannie and built by James Warren, a owner of a nearby sawmill. Henry Lake and Flossie were the last Dickasons to live on the property. Contributed by Merilyn Fleshman.

DICKASON NAMED PRESIDENT BSTC

Succeeds R. P. Sims, Who Will Serve A Business Manager Of Institution; New Head Here For 22 Years

Charleston, W. Va., Aug. 14. (AP) ¬The state board of education appointed today Dean H. L. Dickason as acting president of Bluefield State Teachers college to succeed R. P. Sims, who had served as president for 23 years. Sims was made business manager of the institution

Dickason, a native of Monroe county, has been on the Bluefield faculty for 22 years. He was named on recommendation of the Negro state board of education.

John B. Conn was appointed by the board to substitute for Dr. Drank Barlett, professor of chemistry at Marshall college, who was granted a year's leave of absence. Mrs. Theta Lyon was names to succeed Miss Sue Blondell, se-signed, as home economics instructtor, and Ambrose E. McCaskey, Jr. will assume the post as applied mathematics instructor at Marshall, succeeding Dr. A. G. Bragonier, deceased.

Reproduction of August 16, 1936, Bluefield Daily Telegraph article: "Dickason Named President of BSTC." Bluefield Daily Telegraph, Bluefield, WV, Aug. 16, 1936, Page 10, Craft Memorial Library, Bluefield, WV.

APPROVE DICKASON AS COLLEGE HEAD

Negro Board of Education Recommens Appointment Of Dean H. L. Dickason To Post At Local College

Charleston, W. Va. , Aug. 14. (AP)¬ The Negro state board of education recommended the appointment today pf Dean H. L. Dickason as act ing president of Bluefield State Teachers college to succeed R. P. Sims, who has served for 29 years.

Secretary I. J. K. Wells, who made the announcement, said the appointment is subject to confirmation of the state board of education. He said this was expected when board convenes tomorrow.

Dickason has been associated with the Mercer county institution for 22 years. A native of McDowell county, he holds a master's degree from Ohio State University.

Reproduction of August 15, 1936, Bluefield Daily Telegraph article: "Approve Dickason as College Head" Bluefield Daily Telegraph, Bluefield, WV, Aug. 15, 1936, Page 10, Craft Memorial Library, Bluefield, WV.

Chapter 29 – Politics

When Dr. Sims called Lake into his office in June 1936, Lake assumed that the money was running short again, but he was wrong. His friend and mentor was more somber than usual. "Lake, the board is not rehiring me this year. I wanted you to know immediately." He turned to look out the window, at the train yard and the developing town across the tracks and turned back. "I'm to stay as the business manager. I expect it will in the paper tomorrow."

Lake felt the numbness beginning in his chest. "What? Why?" he asked, then "When?" as it began to sink in.

"Mrs. Sims and I are proud of our accomplishments here. This place will always be part of us, but our goals have been met – beyond our wildest dreams," Dr. Sims spoke softly, "and we will stay as long as we can be useful."

Lake was shaken. He had heard of the gathering political storm against Dr. Sims and wanted no part of it. Times were hard in coal country. People were hungry, businesses were closing and money for education was scarce, all courtesy of the Great Depression. Sims, fighting for the growth of the school, had made enemies who wanted a change in the school's leadership. Their meeting ended with a handshake and Lake's hearty, "Thank you for all you've done for me." By August, Lake had been appointed acting president by the State Board of Education. He was 49 years old.

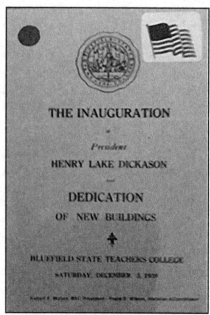

It's official! The Inauguration Program for Henry Lake Dickason's first college presidency. Bluefield State College Archives.

Henry Lake Dickason was ready to lead his own alma mater. He knew the day-to-day routine of the school, every inch of the buildings and grounds, every staff member and every student. His life's work had been spent on the campus and in the communities served by the school. The network and support that he had built over the years strengthened and empowered his leadership. The ideals and philosophies that he'd preached for decades were now visibly guiding him. The view from the front row seat he had occupied during bitter battles fought by President Sims had taught him how to be a warrior for fundraising and a good steward of Bluefield State Teachers College.

He and Flossie moved into the President's House, a modern two-and-a-half story Colonial Revival-style dwelling, connected to Conley Hall by a worn dirt pathway. From the side door, he could gaze straight to the door to the building that held administrative offices. From the front stoop could be seen the lower terrace of the school, with the girls' residence hall first in the line of vision. In this lovely home, with a formal dining room and parlor, Flossie could entertain grandly. One of the first traditions she initiated was a formal welcome for incoming freshmen in the president's home. Some of those young men and women, away from home for the first time, remembered the special reception for the rest of their lives.

---

88 Freshmen Already Enrolled In Local Colored College: Large Squad Practicing For Football Season

Bluefield State Teachers' college opened Tuesday morning, September 8, with prospects for the banner enrollment in its history. To date 88 freshmen have been registered with serveral more expected. According to the registrar, the problem of housing the incoming students is very difficult, and many applications have been refused admission because of the shortage of dormitory facilities

Coach Rowland reports that 48 candidates for the football squad have reported for practice. Of these 48, about 36 are freshmen. This augurs well for a successful season on the gridiron. While the coach refuses to be over optimistic as to the results of the games to be played, the general feeling about the campus is that the opposition for the season will face a well trained, aggressive determined team with it meets Bluefield State Teachers.

Excerpts from an article entitled "BSTC Prospects for Year Bright" in the Bluefield Daily Telegraph, Bluefield, West Virginia, September 13, 1936, details improvements planned by Henry Lake Dickason for the school. Bluefield Daily Telegraph, September 13, 1936, page 10, Craft Memorial Library, Bluefield, WV.

Chapter 30 – Fire

In the first months of his administration, a calamity hit. About three in the morning on Friday, April 23, 1937, a worker at nearby Feuchtenberger Bakery just happened to look out the window and see flames. The main building on campus, Mahood Hall, was on fire. A fire started in the attic of the three-story building. Students in pajamas and bathrobes emptied the dorms and watched the spectacular fire. Firefighters didn't leave until well after 6 o'clock on Saturday. Those first on the scene rescued the athletic trophies from the second floor gymnasium, then the roof caved in and everything else was lost: the auditorium, the library, administrative records, the home economics classrooms, the chemistry lab and a great deal of equipment. Only a shell of three brick walls and the stone foundation remained.

The damage estimate was $150,000 in a time when gasoline cost ten cents a gallon, a new house cost $4,100, and the average monthly rent was $26. There was no insurance and a spokesman for the governing body for the school, the WV State Board of Control, soon announced that they had no money for rebuilding the building. In addition, the whispers had begun that Dr. Dickason was not

> The fire was discovered at 3 o'clock by an employe of the Feuchtenbeger Bakery on Bluefield avenue, who chanced to look out a window and say the flames leaping from the roof of the structure. He gave the alarm, and the fire sirens quickly routed the sleeping students from their domitories nearby. They poured out in pajamas and bathrobes and stood helplessly by watching the flames destroy the building and equipment.
>
> **Library Destroyed**
>
> Only the athletic trophies in the gymnasium on the second floor of the three-story structure, were saved. The roof soon fell in and no one was permitted to enter the building except firemen. The library contained 10,000 volumes and was totally destroyed.

Excerpts from August 15, 1937, Bluefield Daily Telegraph article: "State Officials Inspect Ruins of College Building." Bluefield Daily Telegraph, Bluefield, WV, April 24, 1937, Page 1, Craft Memorial Library, Bluefield, WV.

"Because of the depression and subsequent recession and a disastrous fire, the college facilities are far below what they should be," Dr. Dickason told state authorities. Bluefield State College Centennial History (1895-1995) by C. Stuart McGehee and Frank Wilson.

a good choice for fund-raising because, as a black man, he was not allowed in the upper echelon of Bluefield's wealthy white people where money might be found. He had heard the same whispers during Dr. Sim's administration.

Chapter 31 – Money

Lake pounded his fist on his desk in despair. He needed books and classrooms immediately. The school had needed buildings and land even before the fire. Former President Sims had made that funding his number one priority but had just gotten started.

Dickason's first public responses were to thank the firefighters for the "gallant fight which they made to forestall the loss" and then to assure the community that school could continue and that the summer sessions would be held as scheduled. The community came to the rescue as much as they could but a national recession and cutbacks in the coalfields limited the flow of money in the area. Some teachers worked without paychecks but some left for more stable jobs. Students, faculty, and alumni donated services and cash. The faculty started Bluefield's first Girl Scout Troop and donated their private libraries for student use. Alumni came forth with hundreds of educational volumes to lend to the makeshift library. Sororities and fraternities stepped up with student scholarships. President J. Frank Marsh from Concord College visited from across the county and offered assistance. Between the fire and the ongoing Depression, funds and spirits were low.

Options for financing to keep the school running were limited. However, by June, the number of students enrolled for summer school set a new high and Lake had organized to get money to rebuild. The plans he chose were to lobby the legislature for money and to appeal to wealthy black alumni in northern urban areas.

He went to the capital in Charleston with proof that Bluefield State Teachers College was vital to progress in the

The College attempts to develop two major groups: (A) A group of leaders, and (B) A group capable of being led." Bluefield State College Centennial History (1895-1995) by C. Stuart McGehee and Frank Wilson.

– 103 –

southern part of the state. He compiled data and gave the speech of his life, in part: *Because of the depression and subsequent recession and a disastrous fire, the college facilities are far below what they should be.*

Alumni chapters were notified about their school's need. Members were asked for bequests and contributions. These groups responded: black businessmen and women gave generously.

He was later successful. In 1938, a new gymnasium and 700 seat auditorium, Arter Hall, was completed. It was ready to host Dickason's inauguration ceremony when his appointment from the State Board of Control changed his role from acting president to appointed president. A new wing added to Conley Hall was built to house a modern library. A women's dorm was built, West Hall was leveled and replaced by a new men's residence hall named Payne Hall. Four houses were built for faculty and land was acquired west of U.S. Route 52 on which a Technical Education building was later constructed.

The duties of college president took most of his time during the first few years. The dust and noise of construction were music to his

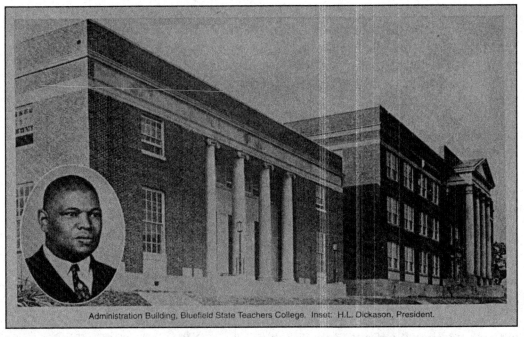

Administration Building, Bluefield State Teachers College. Inset: H.L. Dickason, President.

Conley Hall, the administration building at Bluefield State College looking much like it does today. Inset: Henry Lake Dickason, BSC's first president. Bluefield State College Archives.

ears and he pushed on to make other huge changes, some based on the combined philosophies of Booker T. Washington and W. E. B. Du Bois. As Dickason wrote, "The College attempts to develop two major groups: (A) A group of leaders, and (B) A group capable of being led." Additional programs in business management and secretarial training were added to teaching and liberal arts degree offerings.

Henry Lake Dickason at the podium. Bluefield State College Archives.

Chapter 32 – Family

Lake and Flossie held a party in the president's house for Delbert Dunlap when he finally finished his Master's Degree. Faculty members and alumni attended. Delbert's life, like Lake's, had been dedicated to the education of black students in Bluefield. When Lake had noticed single female teachers showing interest in Delbert, he dared to quietly tease him about finally being ready (at age 52) to get married. Delbert's eyes twinkled and he replied, "All in good time, cousin. We wouldn't want to rush anything, now would we?"

After Bluefield State Teachers College emerged triumphantly from the dark years, Lake and Flossie faced another shadow in their lives, this one personal. It seemed likely that they were unable to have children. Both wanted a child desperately.

They spent most of their time in Bluefield but visited Cismont regularly. Lake bought an older used car at Comer's Chevrolet and agreed on a deal whereby he would drive his shiny black Chrysler DeSoto from Bluefield to Lindside on Friday evening, park it under the garage and drive the used jalopy up the rugged mountain road home. On Sundays, he would reverse the order and drive the big De Soto back to Bluefield. Residents knew to stay clear of his car; he often drove near the middle of the road. The Comer's daughter, Bobbie Jean, played behind the garage as a little girl and many years later would tell about Dr. Dickason's courtesy as he tipped his hat to her when he parked his car.

Lake and Flossie hosted hunting weekends at the farm and invited colleagues from the college as well as those guests visiting. Flossie, with Rose

Henry Lake Dickason in 1937. Bluefield State College Archives.

Hale's help, provided lovely accommodations in their home and a bounteous table for their guests.

After a busy weekend of entertaining guests, Lake found Flossie stretched out in their bed, face buried in the pillow sobbing. "What's causing this?" he asked as he sat down beside her.

"I am so tired, Lake." She rolled onto her side and he could see her face was wet with tears. "Tired and for what? What do we have to show for all the cleaning and cooking?"

"Our guests had a wonderful time, Flossie. They are important men that can help the college."

"Important men with full bellies." She rolled back onto the pillow and pounded it. "College, college, college." She screamed. "I want to do something for us." Again, she cried. He rubbed her back and made shushing sounds and she calmed down enough to sit up and blow her nose. "Lake, I want a family." She hiccuped. "I want our baby, but if it's not meant to be maybe there is a baby out there that needs us." Again she hiccuped. "I want to see about adopting." She looked at him.

He held her tight and whispered in her ear, "Yes, yes, a hundred times yes." She started crying again, for joy.

It didn't take long to find a child that needed them. A beautiful little boy won their hearts completely. He was born in Wheeling, West Virginia in 1935 and was adopted by Fannie and Lake when he was four. Robert Andrew moved into his own room at their home in Bluefield and spent childhood summers and weekends on the farm at Lindside. Flossie was a proud, protective mother and Lake was calmly determined that Bobby would be well educated.

Chapter 33 – Haircut

Even though Lake enjoyed being Bobby's father, there were many responsibilities that went along with being a college president requiring him to be out late or away overnight or even away for several days. Flossie managed Bobby's care without complaint and the active little boy grew into a handsome young man.

Flossie put up with no nonsense especially when it came to Bobby's care. She marched the little boy into Mr. Ingersoll's Monroe County barbershop for a haircut in the early 1940s and announced, "Good afternoon, Mr. Ingersoll, we need Bobby to get a short, neat haircut."

Carl Ingersoll taught at the local high school and cut hair at his barbershop, and he knew immediately that there was going to be trouble. "Mrs. Dickason," he greeted her while mentally weighing his choices, "I don't know how to cut his hair."

"What do you mean you can't cut his hair?" She looked out the window. "That's a barber pole, isn't it?" Mr. Ingersoll nodded. "You're a barber, aren't you?" He nodded again. "Then tell me why you don't know how to cut Bobby's hair."

"I've never cut colored people's hair. I don't know how." Ingersoll felt like if he cut the child's hair incorrectly, Flossie would be even angrier. "I'm sorry, Mrs. Dickason, I can't do it. I can send you to a barbershop out at Ballard."

"Mr. Ingersoll, I think you don't want to wait on us because we are colored." She crossed her

Ingersoll's Barber Shop, a small town business where times were changing more slowly than in urban areas. Library of Congress, Prints & Photographs Division, photograph by John Margolies, LC-MA05- 4755 [P&P].

arms and tapped her foot, staring him down. "You have a barbershop but you won't cut my son's hair."

"No, no, ma'am. I simply don't know how."

"My husband is President of Bluefield State College and he will have your job, sir." She waited and Mr. Ingersoll started sweeping the shop. "You haven't heard the last of this matter." She grabbed Bobby's hand and flounced out the door.

She did mention it to Lake, but Ingersoll remained at his job for many more years.

Chapter 34 – Growth

In 1943, the school's name changed again to reflect the expanding curriculum and campus. Now Bluefield State College, it was impacted in many ways by World War II.

Bluefield State first offered nurse's classes at Providence Hospital, the colored hospital in Bluefield during the war, partly to train military personnel. Summer agricultural training sponsored Victory Gardens, students bought war bonds, and faculty served in the Red Cross and the USO. Nearly 400 alumni served in the military and four active faculty members enlisted. Three students flew with the "Tuskegee Airmen." President Dickason served on the Mercer County Draft board with a his former boss, Mr. Thornton, from Bluefield Hardware.

Professor Joseph E. Dodd designed the College Seal to reflect the change in name from Bluefield State Teachers College to Bluefield State College. Bluefield State College Centennial History (1895-1995) by C. Stuart McGehee and Frank Wilson.

Once again, Lake registered for the draft, at nearly six feet tall and 320 pounds, but at 56 years old, he was not likely to be called. He supported the war effort at home and work and wrote: *To guarantee the defense of the future, education must stay on the march.*

The end of the war and the school's fiftieth anniversary happened during the same year and both were celebrated. Records indicated that 17, 526 students had been served by BSC in the previous 50 years.

The school continued to change with the times. Military men and women returned from service with the GI Bill to help pay for education. In 1949, the school met the requirements of the North

"To guarantee to defense of the future," Dr. Dickason wrote, "education must stay on the march." Bluefield State College Centennial History (1895-1995) by C. Stuart McGehee and Frank Wilson.

Central Association and was granted full accreditation. Centers for in-service training served teachers in fourteen small towns. Classes were offered off-campus at locations across three neighboring counties.

Curriculum was once again modified to include shops for blue-collar training in many areas: carpentry, plumbing, sheet metal, automobile repair as well as service occupations and hotel domestic classes. Six acres west of Route 52 had been obtained earlier and a new concrete building took shape to hold classrooms and labs for the new departments. The building was aptly named Dickason Hall. An entire Division of Vocational Training was to follow.

1940s chemistry classroom at Bluefield State Teachers College. Bluefield State College Archives.

Chapter 35 – Recognition

To say that Henry Lake Dickason was noticed in the black community or in the education community would be an understatement. He was constantly in demand as a speaker for many kinds of organizations including churches, teaching organizations, public schools, and gatherings of his beloved Alpha Phi Alpha. For instance in 1938, he traveled to New Orleans for the general Alpha Phi Alpha convention and spoke to the membership.

A variety of charities and agencies clamored for his leadership and support. He chose those that mattered to him, especially those involving teaching or tuberculosis prevention.

Built during Dr. Dickason's administration, this building housed classrooms for nursing, mining and business classes. It was named Dickason Hall in Dr. Dickason's honor. Bluefield State College Archives.

In the biography of noted Bluefield mathematician John Nash, *A Beautiful Mind*, the author, Sylvia Nasar gave credit to Dr. Dickason when he chaired the Mercer County Draft Board for helping Nash maintain student status. Otherwise Nash would have been drafted during the Korean War and his Nobel Prize winning math theory may not have been created.

His friendships with well-known icons of African-American culture brought national personalities to perform at Bluefield State. Marian Anderson, Leontyne Price, W. C. Handy, (a personal friend), Langston Hughes, and Thurgood Marshall were all guests of Bluefield State and the Dickasons. Heavyweight champion Joe Louis and players from the Negro Baseball League were guests during their exhibition tours.

Dickason was awarded two honorary doctorates, one at Virginia State College in 1942, a Doctorate of Pedagogy and another in 1948 from West Virginia State College, a Doctor of Literary Law. Eleanor Roosevelt was also granted an honorary degree at the same ceremony and spoke at the event. In her journal on May 19, she wrote: *Three of us received honorary degrees – Irvin Stewart, president of West Virginia University; Henry Lake Dickason, president of Bluefield State College; and myself. My address for the occasion was on human rights*

1940s faculty group with Dr. Dickason fourth from left.
Bluefield State College Archives.

Chapter 36 – Robertson

In addition to public service activities, Dr. Dickason supported private individuals in significant ways as well. Perhaps the most lasting recognition for an educator comes from helping a student. William Bernard Robertson, who told his story 65 years after it happened, was one of those students. Although Robertson never spoke with Dr. Dickason after their encounter, his story and the passion with which he tells it is powerful. Robertson declares

I am who I am because of Dr. Dickason.

I am from Roanoke, Virginia. My father and I walked to the train station there on a hot August day in 1950 because I was going to Bluefield to enroll in Bluefield State College. We had looked at colored colleges in North Carolina, but I wanted to go to Bluefield State. When I arrived, I went to Conley Hall to register and after going through the registration process I realized that I didn't have enough money.

I called my father and told him. He said, "There is no more money. Get the next train and come on home. We can check on some of those schools in North Carolina later."

I was in the front of the administration building starting to walk or maybe hitch-hike to the station when the longest car I ever saw stopped in the street and the driver, a portly man, motioned me over. "Where are you bound, young man?" he asked.

I told him, "The train station, can I get a ride?" He told to me get in, so I did.

He drove about thirty yards to a driveway and pulled in. He asked me several questions and found out my situation. "You go on up and register and get a room at the dorm and go to

*my office at nine o'clock tomorrow morning." It was Dr. H. L.
Dickason, president of the college.*

*I was there at 8:30 the next day. This very nice, soft-spoken
man found me a job and let me make payments on my school
fees. When I look back on my life I see that moment as being
providential.*

*I was a senior in college when the U.S. Supreme Court ended
public school segregation but my professors at Bluefield State
had taught me to prepare myself for an integrated world. Those
men and women taught me a great sense of service. Doors
were starting to be opened by Martin Luther King and others
and because I had stood on the shoulders of giants like Dr.
Dickason, I was prepared to enter those doors.*

DR. HENRY LAKE DICKASON shown here speaking. In the background
(left to right) Unknown student; Dr. Theodore Mahaffey and Coach Julius C. Tonsier.

*Dr. Henry Lake Dickason speaking from a church pulpit. In the background (L to R) Unknown
student, Dr. Theodore Mahaffey and Coach Julius C. Tonsier.* Bluefield State College Archives.

I earned two bachelor's degrees at Bluefield State College. I was the one of the first two African-Americans to earn Masters Degrees from Radford University. Over my lifetime, I was awarded three honorary doctorates. The political bug bit me and I ran for the Virginia Assembly. I lost but I didn't really lose because I was appointed as the first African-American to serve on the executive staff of a governor of Virginia.

Robertson served during the administration of President Ronald Reagan as the deputy assistant Secretary of State for African Affairs and visited 65 countries to extend Henry Kissinger's diplomacy. President Gerald Ford appointed him as the Peace Corps director in Kenya. He taught for a while at Virginia Tech and then left at the summons of President Reagan for yet another assignment, assistant director of the U.S. Department of Defense Office of Economic Adjustment.

Robertson headed up a movement to purchase 90 acres near Bedford, Virginia and built a camp for mentally impaired children and adults, Camp Virginia Jaycee, in 1971. He worked within the Booker T. Washington Foundation.

He retired from public service at 69 years of age and used his experience to teach social studies at Hillsborough Middle School in Florida.

Robertson emphasized

None of this would've happened without that hot August day in 1950. When Dr. Dickason saw me afterwards, he'd wave but we never sat down and talked again. After all, he was the president of the school and I was a student. I didn't stay in touch with him after he left and I'm sorry I didn't.

He helped so many of us. I am just one, but I know he did this for others.

Dr. William Robertson, with Dr. Dickason's oil portrait in the "Hall of Presidents" at Bluefield State College. Jim Nelson.

Dr. H. L. Dickason Speaks at Service Of Young People

The highlight of the young people's service of the First Medodist church, Bluefield Va., Sunday morning, as ad address by Dr. H. L. Dickason, president of Bluefield State Teachers college. His subject was "The Negro's Contribution to America."

The speaker gave the white race credit for its attitude toward the negro race in the accomplishment and advancement of the latter. He mentioned a number of members of his race who attained fame and what they contributed to the advancement of America.

Dr. Dickason humorously referred to the Monroe doctrine and stated that he was a native of Monroe county, West Virginia. He was accompanied by Prof. C. O. Ress, head of the music department at the college and Miss Eunice Burwell, who contributed to the musical program. Miss Burwell has a splendid voice. The meeting was held in Palmer Hall.

Reproduction of an article about Dr. Dickason speaking at Methodist church in the Bluefield Daily Telegraph. Bluefield Daily Telegraph, Feb. 10, 1942, page 16, Craft Memorial Library, Bluefield, WV.

Chapter 37 – Lindside

Family members knew that Dr. Dickason would correct language or grammar if improper which made him seem uppity to them at times although his motive was clear; he wanted to improve those around him. Dickason often promoted manners and proper speech and dress. He met his match when correcting a cousin's use of the word "ain't" and lectured Charlie for some time about speaking properly. Charlie Ross stretched out tall and replied with an exaggerated accent, "Well, Lake, I's just talkin' so's *you* could understand me."

Dr. Dickason is remembered in Monroe County as a man that was well aware of the unwritten rules for black and white social interaction. He was respectful to all and respected by all. When a white friend died, Dr. Dickason bought a basket of flowers, went to the man's house and asked his sons playing in the yard if they would take the flowers inside to the widow. It wasn't a matter of courage, he had taken on the WV Legislature and spoke before hundreds of people but he didn't presume to invite himself into the home of a white friend. He was courteous and sensitive to the times.

To William Robertson
With best wishes,
Ronald Reagan

William Robertson shaking hands with former boss, President Ronald Reagan. Jim Nelson.

Flossie may have been ahead of the times. She had her driver stop on the highway between Lindside and Peterstown, U.S. Rt. 219 when she saw a lawn decoration depicting a black jockey holding a lantern. Driving by it week after week (in the 1950s) finally wore her down and she got out and knocked on the owner's door. She explained that it was offensive and the homeowner removed it. Flossie thanked him and drove off.

One local legend tells how dressed up Flossie was at all times. Another is that she subscribed to the daily paper, the Bluefield Daily Telegraph and had it delivered to the closest business, a gas station two miles away in Lindside. She fancied she could tell if the workers at the station had opened it before she picked it up and raised Cain whenever her paper appeared disturbed.

Although Dr. Dickason inspired many students, his son Bobby did not appear inclined to follow in his father's academic footsteps. Bobby had completed Genoa High School in Bluefield and enrolled at Bluefield State while his father was president. He was good-looking and charming, but not as focused on his studies as his parents would have liked. He wanted more freedom and talked his parents into allowing him to move to the dorm rather than live in the President's House with his parents. His social life proved too much of a distraction and he withdrew from classes. Flossie and Lake were unsure how to proceed, but they stood by their son as he tried another school.

Chapter 39 – Resignation

Lake wasn't sure he was ready to retire at age 65 but Flossie couldn't wait to head to the farm with him. She felt the move would lessen the tension he felt on the job. He waited until the end of the 1951-52 school term before he made the announcement. The West Virginia State Board of Education named Dean G. W. Whiting as the acting president. A flurry of events honored Dr. and Mrs. Dickason and they had many moments of pause as they packed and said their goodbyes.

Presentation of a retirement gift to Dr. Dickason on the stage at Arter Hall. Dean Delbert Dunbar with rolled paper and Dr. Dickason (in dark suit) smiling. Bluefield State College Archives.

In their first months back on the mountain, Flossie got a brown dog that she named Sandy, took charge of remodeling and redecorating, and tried new recipes. Lake expanded the herd of cattle and fell back into the patterns of his youth, planning crops and investigating better ways of farming. It was a drastic sudden change in lifestyle but they were adapting fairly well until a phone call came. The President of Morristown College in Tennessee had passed away and his wife, Mary Whitten, had agreed to finish the year. The chairman of the Methodist Episcopal Church Board called to see if Lake was interested in the job.

Morristown had been a regular football and basketball opponent of Bluefield State. It was a historically black school like BSC, but the campus of 365 acres and 14 brick buildings on a hill in northwestern Morristown appealed to Lake after a lifetime of work on the side of a steep hill in Bluefield. "Room to grow," he argued to Flossie who was dead set against the move.

She did agree to visit the school with her husband and they both marveled at its rich history. The college was begun from a grammar school created by a missionary for black students. It became a normal school, seminary, and industrial school. One of the main buildings was a former slave market where some of the first students had been sold. Now, the curriculum was moving away from industrial classes to a more liberal arts school. The buildings, built of student-made bricks fired in a school kiln, were magnificent. Even the long walkways between buildings were covered with long breezy walls fashioned from brick archways.

Lake was sold from the beginning and Flossie knew better than to stand in his way, but she refused to move with him. "I will stay back and run the farm," she announced when she was sure she couldn't change his mind.

Dr. Dickason moved to Tennessee in 1953. He came home during school breaks and spent the summers with her. Flossie visited him as well, but not often. Bobby was living at home with his mother and when he got into a trouble in Lindside, his parents agreed that he would go to Morristown College and enroll. Bobby's heart wasn't in it and his Morristown schooling only lasted a semester. He and his father decided that the military would meet his need for excitement and adventure and he joined the Air Force. He served with the U.S. Air Force in the Philippines.

Dr. Dickason Comes Out Of Retirement To Head College In Tennessee

Dr. H. L. Dickason, one of the nation's leading educators and past president of Bluefield State College, has been named president of Morristown College in Morristown, Tenn.

Dr. Dickason, who has been in retirement for the past year at his farm near Lindside in Monroe County, was president of Bluefield

State College for 16 years. Prior to that he served as teacher, registrar and dean for an aggregate of 38 years of service with the institution.

The announcement of Dr. Dickason's new assignment was made last night by Lynn Sheely, chairman of the board of trustees of Morristown College. He is to succeed the late Miller W. Boyd.

Morristown College is a Methodist institution.

Dr. Dickason, who at one time served as president of the Council of State College and University Presidents, will leave his home today to assume his new duties in Morristown.

While in retirement, Dr. Dickason served as president emeritus of Bluefield State. He is considered one of the leading civic and social workers in this section of West Virginia. During World War II, Dr. Dickason extended his public duties to include a tour of service with the Office of Price Administration in Mercer County and the county draft board.

In church life, Dr. Dickason served as steward of the Methodist Church. He was a representative to the East Tennessee Conference during two general meetings of the group.

Dr. Dickason was elevated to the presidency of Bluefield State in 1937. Following his retirement in July of last year, the State Board of Education paid tribute to the educator for his lengthy and honorable service.

Under his direction, the board said the Bluefield college had reached a ranking position with the nation's top Negro colleges.

Reproduction of an article entitled "Dr. Dickason Comes Out Of Retirement To Head College in Tennessee." Bluefield Daily Telegraph, Septmber 2, 1953, page 2, Craft Memorial Library, Bluefield, WV.

Chapter 40 – Death

At 70 years old, Dr. Dickason should have been slowing down, but there was much to do. His overwork landed him in the Morristown hospital with chest pains. Flossie came, of course, and listened to him fuss about being in the hospital until the pains acted up again. The doctors thought it best to transfer Lake to a larger facility in Knoxville.

According to his death certificate, Dr. Dickason spent two weeks in the hospital before succumbing to a pulmonary infarction on April 6, 1957.

The body of Dr. Henry Lake Dickason lay in state in Arter Hall after a viewing at John Stewart Methodist Church in Bluefield. Hundreds attended his funeral. Newspapers told his story. Countless students and colleagues shared memories of him. His wife and son grieved his loss.

He would not live to bask in the glow of Bluefield State College's continuing success but the school grew and changed with the times as it did when he had led it, offering a quality education to black and white students from southern West Virginia and elsewhere. The curriculum and campus have expanded and adapted to the needs of the area. The Bluefield State College Alumni Association carries on the college mission.

Funeral For Noted Negro Educator Friday

MORRISTOWN, Tenn. AP - Funeral services for Dr. Henry Lake Dickason, president of Morristown College who died in Knoxville last Saturday, will be conducted at the college Friday morning.

Another service for the noted Negro educator will be Sunday afternoon at Bluefield State College, Bluefield, W. Va., where Dr. Dickason was a faculty member for 38 yeras and president for 16.

Dr. Dickason, 70, is survived by his widow and a son, Robert A. Dickason, serving with the U.S. Airforce in the Philippines.

Reproduction of newspaper article detailing services to be held for Dr. Dickason: "Funeral for Noted Negro Educator Friday." Kingsport Times, Kingsport, TN, Apr. 11, 1957.

**Rites Slated Sunday
For Ex-college Head**

Funeral services for Henry L. Dickason, 70, former president of Bluefield State College, will be conducted at 1 p.m. Sunday at the college.

Dickason was president of Bluefield State College from 1936 until his retirement in 1952, and was credited with winning accreditation for the school. He also launched a million dollar building program prior to his retirement.

"Rites Slated Sunday for Ex-College Head" The Raleigh Register, Beckley, WV, Apr. 9, 1957.

Teachers, mining engineers, nurses, and leaders in business and community affairs continue to earn degrees and obtain jobs because of the college.

Henry Lake Dickason was personally influenced by one of America's greatest shames, slavery. His blood ran strong with the courage and perseverance of his grandparents, all four slaves. His life spanned the time when horse-drawn wagons were commonly used to driving his own Chrysler DeSoto coupe. Educationally, Henry Lake soared above the expectation of any parents of the day, white or black.

He walked with dignity in a world of oppression and showed no signs of being oppressed. In a time of harsh racial discrimination, he lived in a white world and followed the rules. He "knew his place" was an intended compliment given sixty years after his death which attempted to describe his humbleness. In a black rural community that was home, he held high expectations of reading and speaking skills.

Although he grew up in the aftermath of the Civil War, he was an adult witness to the resurgence of Black musicians, artists, writers

and athletes. Indeed, he knew many of them personally. And, along with many of his era, he buried family members during the rampages of TB and infection without effective treatment.

Dr. Dickason's final exit from Arter Hall. He was buried at in Oak Grove Cemetery in Bluewell, WV in 1957. Bluefield State College archives.

He stood with his country through World Wars I and II, supported war efforts and served on the local draft board in the 1940s. He lobbied for the education of the underdog. He influenced countless lives by making secondary and higher education relevant.

His faith in God was strong. He led chapel services at the college, was a lay speaker and often found time for prayer.

The life of hard work that Dr. Dickason lived modeled service to others. As he pulled himself up by his bootstraps, he pulled up others: colleagues, students and family members.

Young Lake Dickason took on a challenge that day as he left the security of the family farm to pursue his education. He met that challenge and many more throughout his influential life dedicated to education, diligence, discipline, and integrity. Dr. Dickason championed compassion, racial pride, and high academic standards.

Dr. Henry Lake Dickason was somebody.

Much of the progress of Bluefield State college could be attributed directly to the leadership and administration of Mr. Dickason, who was widly recognized as a leading educator and civic leader.

Hernry L. Dickason was favorably known and respected by all who knew him, of all races, and he took an active paret in Bluefield civic affairs and served on many municipal affairs committees and boards.

. . .

Working almost endlessly, Mr. Dickason had guided the college to its present high standing as a member of the North Central Association of Secondary Schools and Colleges, the American Counsel on Education, and the American Association of Colleges for teacher Education.

Excerpts from an article entitled "Former BSC President Dies" in the Bluefield Daily Telegraph, Bluefield, West Virginia, April 7, 1957. Bluefield Daily Telegraph, Septmber 13, 1936, page 1, Craft Memorial Library, Bluefield, WV.

Appendixes

Dickason Family Trees

United States Census Records 1870

United States Census Records 1880

United States Census Records 1900

United States Census Records 1910

United States Census Records 1940

Last Will & Testament of Jacob Dickason 1875

Guy R. Dickason and Mary F. A Ross Marriage License 1883

Article "Prof. Dickason Joins Old McGuffey Class" 1941

H. L. Dickason's 1917 Draft Registration Card

H. L. Dickason letter to Mariah Dunlap 1911

BCI Athlete's Code

Article "BSTC Prospects Bright" 1937

Article "State Officials Inspect Ruins of College Building." 1937

Jim Nelson Report "William Robertson"

H. L. Dickason Draft Registration Card 1942

H. L. Dickason Public Service Record

Association of Social Science Teachers photograph

Article "Former BSC President Dies" 1957

 H. L. Dickason death certificate 1957

Dr. Dickason's headstone in Bluewell, WV photograph

Dixie Hill Cemetery photographs of Dunlap graves

Jacob Dickason Ancestry

John Dickason . . . . . ⎛ Jacob Dickason   Samuel Augustus Pack . . ⎛ Elizabeth Pack
b
d   b   12/2/1755
       1st appears 1789   d   3/12/1833
       Hardy Co.   m
m   Mary Farley Pack
    Anna Smith   b 1763
     b   d 1832
     d
      Morefield, VA

Jacob Dickason . . . . ⎛ Samuel Dickason
b   8/18/1789   b   1815
d   11/18/1879   d   6/15/1829
     Rockingham, VA - Lindside, WV
m
    Elizabeth (Betsey) Pack
     b 10/3/1781
     d 1/9/1867

Jacob Dickason's Heirs (Former Slaves)

    Raeburn Hall Dickason . . . . . . See next page
    b   1827
    d   3/30/1917
    m
      Nancy Jane Pack
       b 9/1822
       d 8/4/1888

    James Dickason . . . . See next page
    b   8/1/1847
    d   11/6/1912
    m   12/4/1863
      Jennie Lyn Shanklin
       b 3/12/1851   ⎛ Mary Dickason
       d 7/9/1909   b   1860
                              d
    Lewis Dickason . . . .
    b   Lewis Dickason
    d   1917   b   1873
    m   d
      Juda Peck Dickason
       b 1823   Ida Dickason
       d 1908   b   1867
                              d

James Dickason and Descendants

James Dickason . . . .
b 8/1/1847
d 11/6/1912
m 12/4/1863
    Jennie Lyn Shanklin
      b 3/12/1851
      d 7/9/1909

Lottie Elizabeth Hill
b 7/21/1869
d 10/21/1826

Homer H. Dickason
b 3/11/1876
d 2/20/1903

Abbie Garfield Ross
b 1/14/1851
d 2/3/1936

Raeburn Hall Dickason and Descendants

Raeburn Hall Dickason . . . . . .
b 1827
d 3/30/1917
m
    Nancy Jane Pack
      b 9/1822
      d 8/4/1888

Margaret Carter Dickason
b 1849
d 1928

Fanny Dickason
b 1851
d

John Woodson Dickason
b 1850
d 1930

Nancy Jane Hall
b 1852
d

Hugh C. Dickason
b 1855
d 1927

Shedrick Dickason
b 1860
d 1955

Isaiah Dickason
b 1861
d 1930

Guy R. Dickason . . . . . . see next page
b 1865
d 1929

Guy R. Dickason and Descendants

Guy R. Dickason . . . .
b   1865
d   1929
m 12/18/1883
    Mary Fannie Ross
       b 1866
       d 1933

Hattie Dickason
b   4/9/1885
d   2/5/1895

Bernard French (Bernie) Dickason
b   1899
d   1923

Henry Lake Dickason . . .
b   1886
d   1957
m 1919
    Gracie Robinson
       b 1882
       d 1919
m 1932
    Flossie Mack
       b 1904
       d 1978

Henry Lake Dickason, Jr.
b   1915
d   1915
Robert Andrew Dickason
(adopted)
b   1969
d   2000
m
    Pat

Early Census Information

Red Sulphur Spring, Monroe County, WV Census						
October 15, 1870						
Name	Age	Sex	Color	Occupation	Birth	Citizenship
Dickison, Jacob	69	M	W	Farmer	VA	US

Red Sulphur District, Monroe County, WV Census								
June 17, 1880								
Surname	Name	Race/ Gender	Age	Rel.	Occupation	Birth	Father Birth	Mother Birth
Dickison	Reanburn	B/Male	53		Farmer	VA	VA	VA
	Nancy	B/Female	57	Wife	Keeping house	WV	VA	WV
	Guy	B/Male	23	Son	Farm laborer	WV	VA	WV
	Shederick	B/Male	14?	Son	Farm laborer	WV	VA	WV
	Isaiah	B/Male	16	Son	Farm Laborer	WV	VA	WV

This 1880 Census record shows Raburn and Nancy Dickason, Henry Lake's grandparents, and their household. Census takers often took liberties with spellings, hence, Raburn, Rayburn, Raenburn, and Raeburn may all refer to the same citizen.

Early Census Information

Red Sulphur District, Monroe County, WV Census									
June 7, 1900									
Name		Relationship	Race	Sex	Age	Birth	Occupation	Can read	Can write
Dickinsen	Guy F.	Head	B	M	42	WV	farmer	yes	yes
	Fannie	wife	B	F	33	WV	-	yes	yes
	Henry L.	son	B	B	13	WV	farm laborer	yes	yes
	Bernie F.	son	B	B	1	WV	-	-	-

Milner District, Georgia Census									
April 19, 1910									
Name		Relation-ship	Sex	Race	Age	Single/Married	Occupation	Birth	Read and write
Mack	Henry	Head	M	B	27	M	Farmer	GA	Yes
	Ophelia	wife	F	Mu	25	M	None	GA	Yes
	Flossie J.	daughter	F	Mu	6	S	None	GA	-

Bluefield City, WV Census								
Bluefield Teachers College								
April 19, 1940								
Name	Relationship	Sex	Race	Age	Highest level of school	Birth	Occupation	Income
Dickason, Henry	Head	M	Neg	54	C-5	WV	Vice-President Colored College	$3549
Dickason, Flossie M.	Wife	F	Neg	35	C-5	Georgia	-	0

Next Pages
The Last Will & Testament of Jacob Dickason shows that all his worldly possessions were left to former slaves. This was unusual and infers a likewise unique closeness between slaves and property owner. It is known that the former slaves and their families settled here and created a community. In addition, Raeburn Hall Dickason was appointed executor of the estate. Jacob Dickason will dated June 22, 1875, Monroe Co. Wills, Book 11, page 537.

witnesses thereto, and the same is ordered to be recorded.

Teste-

A. A. Nickell, Clerk.

In the name of God Amen, I Jacob Dickason of the County of Monroe and State of West Virginia do make this my last will and testament as follows to wit.

1st I give to my former Slave James Dickason (Colored) The tract of land where he now lives Containing by recent survey made by S. Y. Symms One Hundred and thirty five acres be the same more or less with the appurtenances thereto belonging and bounded as follows beginning at a black oak and chestnut stump at the end of the lane corner to E. P. Fleshmans land N 44 W 23 poles to a white oak root corner to A. L. Fleshman N 32 E 56 poles to two white oaks S 87 E 94 Poles to a white oak corner to Jno. Shultz S 27 E 101 Poles to a double chestnut S 27 W 66 poles to no Sugar Trees S 54 W 29 poles passing large chestnut corner on Manns line to a chestnut N 29 West 43 poles to a Lynn S 45 W 87 poles to a poplar N 34 W 45 poles to a dogwood N 14 W 15 poles to a Stake N 12 W 69 Poles to a double chestnut Stump by the road N 71 E 14 poles to the begining I also give to said James Dickason (Colored) My Rifle Gun and all the property belonging to me now in his possession Except One picded Cow.

2nd I give and bequeath to my former Slave Lewis Dickason (Colored) Seventy two acres of land where he now lives recently surveyed by S. Y. Symms with appurtenances thereto belonging being bounded as follows beginning at a Lynn near the road and running S 37 E 20 poles to a plum bush S 31 E 13 poles to an ash S 52 W 50 poles to a bunch of maples on Simeon Raines line & with the same S 70 E 16 poles to two lower woods S 30 E 74 poles to two chestnuts N 69 E 44 poles to a large Spanish oak N 52 E 61 poles to a Stake in a hollow near a big rock N 37 W 85 poles to a Sugar tree by the road N 71 W 28 poles to a chestnut West 30 poles to the begining. I also give and bequeath to said Lewis Dickason The yoke of Cattle and bay mare that are now in his possession and all the farming tools cooking vessels & other property furnished by me now in his possession I also give him.

3rd I give and bequeath to my former Slave Hugh Dickason, cold, son of Reaburn the tract of land I recently bought of Woodson Cummins Containing Seventy acres be the same more or less with this reservation that is to say I reserve One half of the [ ] that may grow on said tract of land for the use and benefit [of] father Reaburn and family during the lifetime of Reaburn,

4th I give to Fanny Dickason Daughter of Reaburn One milch Cows to be selected by my Executor.

5th The residue of my property both real and personal give & bequeath to my former Slave Reaburn Dickason (Cold) called Raburn Hall) including the residue of my lands live sto[ck] House hold Kitchen furniture bonds money and every other spe[cies] of property not already disposed of Out of which I desir[e] my funeral Expenses shall be paid.

6th I hereby constitute and appoint said Reaburn Dickas[on] (Colored) Executor of this my last will and testament revoking [all] other wills heretofore made by me In testimony whereof I ha[ve] hereunto affixed my hand and Seal this the 22nd day of June [A.D.] 1875.

Jacob Dickason [Seal]

Signed Sealed and acknowledged
by Jacob Dickason as his last
Will and testament in our presence
    Wm McClaugherty
    C. A. Black
    R. N. Spangler
    Lewis Ballard

West Va. In Monroe County Court Clerks Office
                November 26th 187[ ]

A paper purporting the last Will and Testament of Jacob Dickas[on] decd was presented in this office this day and proved by the oath of William McClaugherty and C. A. Black. subscribing witness[es] thereto and the same is ordered to be recorded; And thereupo[n] Reaburn Dickason (Cold) the Executor therein named appear[ed] who made oath thereto, and together with James A. Dickason (C[old]) & Hugh Dickason (Cold) as his securities entered into and ack[nowl-]edged a bond in the penalty of $2000.00 with Condition accor[ding] to law. Certificate for obtaining a probate of said Will in [due] form is granted him.
            Teste –   A. A. Nickell, Clerk.

Marriage License.

West Virginia, County of Monroe, to wit:

To any Person Licensed to Celebrate Marriage:

You are hereby authorized to join together in the Holy State of Matrimony, according to the rules and ceremonies of your Church or religious denomination, and the laws of the State of West Virginia, Guy R. Dickason (cold) and Mary F. A. Ross (cold)

Given under my hand, as Clerk of the County Court of said County, this 15th day of December 1883

A. A. Nickell Clerk.

Certificate to Obtain a Marriage License.

To be Annexed to the License, Required by Chapter 63, Code.

Preliminary inquiries and answers thereto, made and ascertained by A A Nickell Clerk of the County Court of Monroe County, State of West Virginia, relative to Mr. Guy R. Dickason of Monroe County and State of West Virginia, and Miss Mary F. A. Ross of Monroe County, and State of West Virginia, to whom the accompanying Marriage License is issued.

THE FULL NAMES OF THE PARTIES ARE AS FOLLOWS:

His full name is Guy R. Dickason
Her full name is Mary Fannie A. Ross
His age is 24 Years
Her age is 17
He was born in Monroe County, State of West Virginia
She was born in " County, State of
His place of residence is " County, State of
Her place of residence is " County, State of
The name of the party giving the foregoing information Wesley Ross, of Monroe County, State of WVa

Given under my hand, this 15th day of December 1883

A. A. Nickell Clerk County Court.

Minister's Return of Marriage.

I Certify, That on the 14th day of December 1883, at the house of Banks Ross I united in Marriage the above named and described parties, under authority of the annexed License.

Rev C. S. Campbell

NOTE—The Minister or other person celebrating such marriage, shall, within sixty days thereafter, return the said license to the office whence it issued, with an indorsement thereon of the fact of such marriage, and the time and place of celebrating the same, under penalty of forfeiture of his bond.

Slave marriages were not always documented, but that of Fannie Ross and Guy R. Dickason left behind a certificate complete with a note from Fannie's guardian allowing her to marry at 17. Monroe County Courthouse, Union, WV.

PROF. DICKASON JOINS OLD McGUFFEY CLASS

The appended letter is from Prof. H. L. Dickason, president of Bluefield State Teachers college will be read with interest. Both the writer and Prof. Dickason were born at Lindside. The head of the Bluefield State Teachers college comes from a family of educators. We are glad to enroll Dr. Dickason in the class of yesterday. His letter follows:

"I read, with interest, your contributions to the Bluefield Telegraph. Those contributions touching Monroe county are of particular interest to me because I was born, and grew up at Lindside.

"It is interesting to read about the McGuffy club.

"I do not know what the qualifications for membership are, but I happen to have a McGuffey speller, McGuffey second reader and a McGuffey third reader.

"When I was studying these over in Monroe, I had some other books that went along with these readers and spellers. I have the following that I studied way back then. Kenneys' Geography of West Virginial Mongomery's Beginner; American History; Harvey's Elementary grammer, and composition; Cutter's Beginners Intermediate Anatomy; Physiology and Hygiene.

"To be sure these bring back pleasant memories when 'Faith was fair and Hope was sure.'

The letter is signed by H. L. Dickason.

We learn that Mr. Dickason owns the old home place near Lindside and visits his old home now and then. He was over there this past weekend.

Dr. Dickason never forgot his early education and the materials used to teach reading to his contemporaries. Reproduction of an article from the Bluefield Daily Telegraph.
Bluefield Daily Telegraph, Feb. 21, 1941, page 6, Craft Memorial Library, Bluefield, WV.

Front and back of Henry Lake Dickason's 1917 draft registration card. The U.S. National Archives and Records Administration, Atlanta, GA.

Dear Aunt "Mer:-
I was glad to receive a letter from you all and to know you all were doing well. I often think of Monroe and especially that good buttermilk that you always have. I have not had anything in the way of good buttermilk, good butter and good pies since I left Monroe in September.

I am kept quite busy at my studies we have from twenty-five to fifty pages at every recitation and it is not a matter

of having an idea about the lessons but they must be so thoroughly known, that often visitors are asked to come to class and the Profs. then sometimes call on any of us to explain the first five or ten pages intelligibly to the visitor.

Some days I go to class at eight o'clock and some days at ten and get out at twelve and two.

I am glad both the children at home and those in school at Bluefield are doing so well. I should think that you are planning to see Delbert get his "sheep skin" in June. I should suppose it is a source of pleasure for parents when two or three of their children are getting educations which will be of so much benefit to all concerned and who stand in so great esteem as your children do with the school authorities especially at Bluefield.

Letter written to his Aunt Mariah Dunlap by H. L. Dickason in 1911. This document was shared with The Monroe Watchman, Union, WV, by Ms. Justine Nall, of Union and published June 18, 2015.

3.

Tell Uncle Elijah that he
is equalling these Ohio farmers
in finishing his plowing so
early. I should think he
will have a good crop as he
is beginning so early. Is
Lizzie going to keep him from
coming to the Springs.

Well I suppose mamma
will come up by and by she
does not write much for I
have rec'd a letter and a card
from her since Christmas
I don't know why she is so
slow about writing. I write
real often to them well I suppose
they are busy.

4

Uncle Joe is foreman on
the street also he has two
teams going very regularly.
He makes good money but
it requires so much for
a living here. Aunt Alice's
birthday was yesterday Apr. 1
she talks of going to Ronceverte
to see Aunt Ann Banks some
time this spring. Summer
is practicing medicine
at Lima Ohio. He is married
I room with Martha Parker
she has a nice house. Her husband makes good money.
Room rent out here is very high
costing from $5.00 to $7.50 per month.

5.

There are nearly three thousand students in the University and about
28 colored. Only two in the University
from Columbus. It seems a great
pity that these colored folks here do
not take advantage of their envi-
ronments.

It was a great pity that
Booker Washington was assaulted the
other day for it has almost ruined
the race. For the facts are very
much different from what most
of the papers relate. As the leading negro of the country what he
does affects the mass of Negroes.

Does Mrs Lilly & Mr Ruddell
keep well? I do not know her but
hearing you talk so much of her it
seems that I know of her also.

Remember me to every one
whom I know also remember me
in your prayers.
Did you all get a new pastor?
            Your Nephew
            H. L. Dickason

1310 Summit St.   4/2/11.
Columbus. Ohio.

An Athlete's Code

We, Blueflield Institute's athletes, believe and practice the following principles in all our games:

1. We accept defeat in the spirit that we lost to a better team and have always a cheer and handshake for our victors.

2. We accept defeat in the spirit that we lost to a better team and have always a cheer and handshake for our victors.

3. We do not dispute or argue or question the decisions of any official, nor do be blame them for the games we lose.

4. We do not believe tht it hurts us to be beaten by any team; therefore, we are always ready to compete with the strongest and the best.

5. We believe that the school and the team is greater than any man or player, so, the best we have is what we give in every minute of every practice and every game.

6. It is our aim to be gentlemen on the field and off the field and we tolerate no cheats, cowards, or muckers in our midst.

BCI athletes were expected to follow the school's Athletic's Code. Bluefield State College Centennial History (1895-1995) by C. Stuart McGehee and Frank Wilson.

BSTC PROSPECTS FOR YEAR BRIGHT

88 Freshmen Already Enrolled In Local Colored College: Large Squad Practicing For Football Season

Bluefield State Teachers' college opened Tuesday morning, September 8, with prospects for the banner enrollment in its history. To date 88 freshmen have been registered with serveral more expected. According to the registrar, the problem of housing the incoming students is very difficult, and many applications have been refused admission because of the shortage of dormitory facilities.

Coach Rowland reports that 48 candidates for the football squad have reported for practice. Of these 48, about 36 are freshmen. This augurs well for a successful season on the gridiron. While the coach refuses to be over optimistic as to the results of the games to be played, the general feeling about the campus is that the opposition for the season will face a well trained, aggressive determined team with it meets Bluefield State Teachers.

Some of the teams on this year's schedule are: Virginia State, Kentucky State, Hampton, Morgan, North, Carolina, A. & T., North Carolina State and Wilberforce. The opening home game will be with Kentucky State on the 3rd of October. The season's thriller will be West Virginai State at Bluefield Bowl early in November. Already the Big Blues are pointing for this game with the war cry, "We will win."

Every student is looking forward to next Friday night, when according to reports, a student mix will be the program of the evening. Music will probably be furnished by Nelson's Night Hawks and dancing will be the order of the evening from 8 until late.

President Dickason is apparently determined to see that everything is done for the comfort and conventence of the students. He is to be seen everywhere about the campus inquiring as to their welfare and planning for their comfort and convience. One of the new things planned is a telephone in the boy's dormitory, a much needed conventence, with a reasonable amount of co-operation from everyone Bluefield State Teachers' college will go far under his administration.

Reproduction of Bluefield Daily Telegraph article: "BSTC Prospects for Year Bright."
Bluefield Daily Telegraph, Bluefield, WV, April 24, 1937, Page 1, Craft Memorial Library, Bluefield, WV.

STATE OFFICIALS INSPECT RUINS OF COLLEGE BUILDING

Asset They Are In No Position To Predict Replacement Of Structure

DAMAGE IS PLACED AT $150,000 BY BOARD

Fire Chief, However, Says Damage Less, Due to Fact Building Was Put Up More Than 30 Years Ago; Blaze Was Spectacular

State officials who came here ???? to investigate the fire that destroyed Mahood Hall on the campus of Bluefield State Teachers college during the early hours of Friday morning, entailing a loss estimated at $150,000, said they were in no position now to make any statement regarding replacement of the structure, one of the oldest of the institution's buildings.

After spending several hours going over the ruins in company with Parker J. Wilson, of the state fire marshal's office, who came from his headquarters in Princeton early yesterday morning. M. D. Carrico, secretary and C. P. Nelson, of the state board of control, departed for Charleston. They said they would make their report to the board at an early date.

Owing to a lack of funds and no insurance, members of the state board of control did not speak in optimistic terms regarding an imediate restoration of the building. During their visit to Bluefield they conferred with A. B. Mahood., local architect, who had designed two wings which were added to this structure in recent years.
Small Salvage

Mr. Mahood said that the salvage from the building would not be a great item. He was authorized to compile estimates on the salvage and file it with the board of control as soon as possible. The local architect said that the four walls, all that remains of the structure, asisde from the rock foundation, would have to be torn away.

Fire Chief E. E. McClure's estimates on the loss were fixed at a figure no greater thatn one-third the amount estimated by John Itaker White, president of the state board of control. White said the construction cost of the building was $133,114. He valued the library and physical equipment at $40,000.
$50,000 Value

McClure said that due to the fact that the main part of this building was erected in 1896, and that the two wings added in later years were not of fireproof construction,he estimate on the actual present day value of the structure and its contents would probably not exceed $50,000.

The fire was discovered at 3 o'clock by an employe of the

Feuchtenbeger Bakery on Blue-field avenue, who chanced to look out a window and say the flames leaping from the roof of the structure. He gave the alarm, and the fire sirens quickly routed the sleeping students from their dom-itories nearby. They poured out in pajamas and bathrobes and stood helplessly by watching the flames destroy the building and equipment.

Library Destroyed

Only the athletic trophies in the gymnasium on the second floor of the three-story structure, were saved. The roof soon fell in and no one was permitted to enter the building except firemen. The li-brary contained 10,000 volumes and was totally destroyed.

Fire Chief McClure said that when the call came in he at once realized that it the fire had gained any headway firemen would be helpless to save the structure. Dur-recent months, he said, he had (Turn to Page Ten)

INSPECT RUINS OF COLLEGE BUILDING

(Continued From Page One)

brought to the attention of the school that there was only a four-inch main running from Park street to the campus, which is ap-proximately 2,000 feet away, and the water supply, which is a dead end main, was entirely inadequate to combat a fire of any conse-quence.

He futher state that he had run tests with tone of the pumpers to demonstrate that even with this auxiliary service that the pressure was entirely too light to furnish adequate service to the buildings.

Two Hose Lines

During the three-hour fight that the firemen staged under great difficulties they were only able to use two lines of hose. The serial tower was attempted but when this was placed in service it was necessary to cut off one of the other lines

McClure said that had the pres-sure been available his men would have been able to have saved two of the wings and a part of the main unit, despite the fact that the fire had gained a big headway in the roof before it was discovered.

The fire chief id not criticize the school faculity, say that they has shown disposition to co-operate and had recently placed an order for a fire alarm boc to be installed on the campus. McClure said they had done this at he sug-guestion, pointing to the fact that a quick alarm would probably en-able firemen to extinguish a blaze with what pressure was available on the campus.

Started in Attic

Reports yesterday that the fire had probably started in the chem-ical laboratory were denied by Chief McClure, who said that this department was one of the last to burn. While he was uncertain as to the origin he said that there was no question as to what part of the building the fire broke out-- the attic. Various school equipment was stored in the attic.

Firemen plays a stream of water on the ruins until 6 o'clock last evening. The visited the scene at intervals throughout the night, giving the smouldering ruins a new drenching each visit.

H. L. Dickason, president of the college, stressed the fact yesterday that the fire will in no way hinder plans for the summer term.

Named for Princeton

Mahood Hall was erected in 1896 and for a time served as the administration and classroom building. In 1904 it was enlarged and in 1926 two wings were built on by the state. It was named in honor of Senator William Maitland Mahood, of Princeton, who was instrumental in passing a bill in the state legislature which created the college.

It wsa just thitry years ago today that Senator Mahood, who died in El Paso, Texas, where he had gone in search of health, was buried in his home city, the Mercer county seat.

In Mahood Hall was the college library, the college auditorium and gymnasium, the college department of home economics and chemistry laboratory, seven roons on the back were utilized for the Clenoa senior high school, taught by teacher training students of the college.

The office of the PWA superintendent on the new boys' dormitory, which is being erected on the campus, was also located in Mahood Hall. All of his records were destroyed.

Accepting the figures of the state officials, McClure said that Bluefield's fire loss in the last three days had exceeded the total annual fire loss in the city of Bluefield for the past twelve years. Should yesterday's loss stand at $150,000 Bluefield's total fire loss this week reached $171,000.

The total loss last year was $112,439. For the preceding ten years the annual loss in no one year exceeding $65,000, ranging from that figure to the small sum of $10,765. In 1925 the total loss in the city was $242,331. That was the year that Beaver high school burned.

During January, February and March of 1937 the total loss was $3,417.

Reproduction of August 24, 1937, Bluefield Daily Telegraph article: "State Officials Inspect Ruins of College Building." Bluefield Daily Telegraph, Bluefield, WV, April 24, 1937, Page 1, Craft Memorial Library, Bluefield, WV, Craft Memorial Library, Bluefield, WV.

Jim Nelson Report

More than 60 years ago, a tall, slender young man from modest means walked onto the 40-acre campus of Bluefield State College. It felt to him that he had stepped into a new world.

The campus, although small by traditional standards, was huge to the young man from the Roanoke Valley of Virginia. The students were well dressed, the faculty expected a lot from them, and the courses were demanding.

To William Bernard Robertson, it was intimidating and he felt out-of-place. Understandably, he was homesick….so, after just a few days at B.S.C., he scraped together his remaining few dollars and went to the Bluefield train station to purchase a ticket and return to his home.

While he waited at the station, fate intervened in the form of a large distinguished-looking gentleman who drove up in a long, black automobile. The man was Dr. Henry Lake Dickason, the president of Bluefield State College. He asked young William Robertson what he was doing, and when he learned that the student was going to return home…. Dr. Dickason offered the young student a ride back to campus, set him up with meals and a place to stay, and instructed him to come to the president's office the following Monday.

That day, more than 60 years ago, changed William Robertson's life forever. "He arranged for me to get a job so I could afford tuition, and he gave me some fatherly advice," Dr. Robertson recalled during a program in his honor at BSC a few years ago. Inspired by that lecture that mixed encouragement and tough love in equal measure, young William Robertson went on to earn two degrees at BSC and he began a lifetime of service. All along the way, he passed along to others the gift of wisdom, direction, and encouragement he had received from Dr. Dickason.

As a member of the Roanoke, Virginia Jaycees, he embraced a service project that no one else wanted—mental retardation. He led a drive to raise money to start a recreational camp, Camp Virginia Jaycee, that has grown to 90 acres and has served more than 34,000 differently-abled adults since its establishment.

Dr. Robertson's civic success caught the eye of Virginia gubernatorial candidate Linwood Holton. When Holton was elected governor, he hired Robertson as the first African-American assistant to the governor in Virginia's history.

He served on President Richard Nixon's committee on mental retardation, representing the president at hundreds of speeches and traveling to more than 50 nations.

In 1975, he was appointed director of the Peace Corps for Kenya. Ultimately, he served four U.S. presidents.

When he graduated from Bluefield State College, he started teaching in a one-room school in Wyoming County. Several years ago, he returned to the classroom, joining the faculty at Sligh Middle School in Tampa, Florida. He's a beacon of hope for the students, and each summer, he travels back to his alma mater in Bluefield, accompanied by several of his Sligh Middle School students, and his message to them is similar to the message Dr. Dickason delivered to young William Robertson more than 60 years ago……

Dr. Dickason's WWII Draft card provides personal information as well as his classic signature. *Ancestry.com.*

H. L. Dickason Community Service

- Alpha Phi Alpha (National General Secretary 1913, National General President 1914, Committee on Standards Chair, 1933-42)
- Bluefield City Draft Board (Member)
- Carolina Community House (Director)
- Curriculum Committee on Teacher Education for West Virginia (Member)
- Greater Bluefield Community Chest (Director)
- Greenbrier-Monroe County Tuberculosis and Health Association (Board of Directors)
- McDowell-Mercer Teachers Roundtable (President and Treasurer)
- Mercer County Draft Board (Member and Secretary)
- Mercer County Tuberculosis and Health Association (Director)
- Methodist Church (Member, John Stewart Methodist Church, Steward, Delegate to Annual Conference, Member of the Jurisdictional Conference, Member of the General Board of Education and the General Quadrennial Emphasis Commission of the Church, Vice-President of the Baltimore Area Council, and the President of the Board of Missions of the East Tennessee Conference)
- National Freedom Day Program in Philadelphia (Represented West Virginia for six years)
- Office of Price Administration during WWII (Member)
- West Virginia Curriculum Committee on Teacher Education
- West Virginia Council of College Presidents (President)
- West Virginia State Teachers Association (President and Historian)
- WV Interracial Housing Commission (Member)
- "Work and Pray" (Vocalist on collection of Historic Negro Spirituals and Work Songs from West Virginia, 2003, WV University Press)

Association of Social Science Teachers in Negro Colleges, Dr. Dickason is front row, second from right.
Bluefield State College Archives.

Former BSC President Dies

Henry L. Dickason, about 70, died in University Hospital at Knoxville, Tenn. about 6 p.m. yesterday. Death was attributed to a heart ailment.

Mr. Dickason was president of Bluefield State college from 1936 until his retirement in 1952, and shortly after retiring as Bluefield State president he became president at Morristown College in Tennessee, a position he held at the time of his death.

H. L. Dickason received his A.B. and M.A. degrees from Ohio State University and joined the faculty of Bluefield State college in 1916??, then known as Bluefield Colored Institute. He served as teacher, registrar and dean before he became president.

Leading Educator

Much of the progress of Bluefield State college could be attributed directly to the leadership and administration of Mr. Dickason, who was widly recognized as a leading educator and civic leader.

Hernry L. Dickason was favorably known and respected by all who knew him, of all races, and he took an active paret in Bluefield civic affairs and served on many municipal affairs committees and boards.

Dr. Dickason became ill several weeks ago but was thought to be improving in recent days. He spent a few days in the Morristown hospital, then was transferred to University hospital in Knoxville.

He is survived by his widow, the former Flossie Mack of Atlanta, Ga. who is the only close survivor.

Henry Lake Dickason was a native of Monroe county and own ed a farm in that county to which he retired after leaving his Bluefield State college post. However, he was soon called to Morristown College as its president and during the few years he served at that institution he was credited with many improvements at the school.

In 1951, H. L. Dickason was elected president of the state colleges and university presidents in this state. He also served as president of the West Virginia State Teacher's association, as its historian for 16 years and was president of the Mercer-McDonwell Round Table, its treasurer for 12 years, a member of the curriculum committee on teacher education for West Virginia.

Church Leader

He was a seward of the Methodist church here, a representative to the East Tennessee conference at several general conferences of the Methodist church.

In civic affairs in Bluefield, H. L. Dickason served as a member of the price panel of the OPA and the selective service board, and a member of the Interracial Housing Commission of West Virginia. He was also on the board of directors of the Community Chest.

He was selected by three different governors as one of two

representatives of the state to the National Freedom Day celebration held annually in Philadelphia.

Bluefield State College was an unaccredited institution when Mr. Dickason took over its helm in 1936. He as beset by many dificulties in the early years of his administration. The building which housed the college library, high school department, gum and auditorium burned.

Working almost endlessly, Mr. Dickason had guided the college to its present high standing as a member of the North Central Association of Secondary Schools and Colleges, the American Counsel on Education, and the American Association of Colleges for teacher Education. The college educational program has been expanded to include liberal arts in addition to teacher education.

One of his last projects here was a million dollar building program that he saw to successful conclusion. A vocational building and a health and physical education' building was included among those projects.

Funeral arrangements are incomplete.

Reproduction of an article entitled "Former BSC President Dies" in the Bluefield Daily Telegraph, Bluefield, West Virginia, April 7, 1957. Bluefield Daily Telegraph, Septmber 13, 1936, Craft Memorial Library, Bluefield, WV.

4709
.28
3292
BIRTH NO.

DEPARTMENT OF PUBLIC HEALTH **CERTIFICATE OF DEATH** DIVISION OF VITAL STATISTICS
STATE OF TENNESSEE
DEATH NO. 57-09182

1. NAME	HENRY	LAKE	DICKASON	2. DATE OF DEATH	4	6	57
	FIRST	MIDDLE	LAST		MONTH	DAY	YEAR

3. COLOR OR RACE N	4. SEX M	5. SINGLE, MARRIED, WIDOWED, DIVORCED (SPECIFY) MARRIED	6. DATE MONTH DAY YEAR OF BIRTH 9-9-86	7. AGE IN YEARS LAST BIRTHDAY) 70	IF UNDER 1 YR. MONTHS DAYS	IF UNDER 24 HRS. HOURS MINS.

8. PLACE OF DEATH
A. COUNTY KNOX
B. CIVIL DISTRICT
C. CITY OR TOWN KNOXVILLE, TENNESSEE
D. LENGTH OF STAY IN THIS PLACE APPROX. 2 WKS.
E. NAME OF HOSPITAL OR INSTITUTION U. T. HOSPITAL
F. INSIDE CITY LIMITS? YES ☒ NO ☐

9. USUAL RESIDENCE OF DECEASED (Where Deceased Lived. If Institution, Residence Before Admission)
A. STATE TENN. B. COUNTY HAMBLEN. CIVIL DISTRICT
C. CITY OR TOWN MORRISTOWN, TENNESSEE
E. INSIDE CITY LIMITS? YES ☒ NO ☐
F. STREET ADDRESS (OR LOCATION)
G. IS RESIDENCE ON A FARM? YES ☐ NO ☐

10A. USUAL OCCUPATION PRESIDENT	10B. KIND OF BUSINESS OR INDUSTRY COLLEGE SCHOOL	11. SOCIAL SECURITY NUMBER	12. WAS DECEASED EVER IN U.S. ARMED FORCES? YES, NO, OR UNKNOWN NO IF YES, GIVE WAR OR DATES OF SERVICE NONE
13. BIRTHPLACE (State or Foreign Country) WEST VIRGINIA	14. CITIZEN OF WHAT COUNTRY? UNITED STATES	15. NAME OF HUSBAND OR WIFE (MRS) FLOSSIE MACK DICKASON	
16. FATHER'S NAME GUY DICKASON	17. MOTHER'S MAIDEN NAME FANNIE ROSS	18. INFORMANT Mrs. H. L. Dickason	ADDRESS Morristown, Tennessee

MEDICAL CERTIFICATION
46ᵗʰ
INTERVAL BETWEEN ONSET AND DEATH

19. CAUSE OF DEATH
PART 1. DEATH WAS CAUSED BY:
IMMEDIATE CAUSE (A) *Pulmonary Infarction* undeter
Conditions, if any, which gave rise to above causes (A); stating the underlying cause last
DUE TO (B) *Pulmonary Embolus*
DUE TO (C)

PART II. OTHER SIGNIFICANT CONDITIONS CONTRIBUTING TO THE DEATH BUT NOT RELATED TO TERMINAL DISEASE CONDITION GIVEN IN PART I (A) *Myocardial infarction* 420
20. WAS AUTOPSY PERFORMED? YES ☐ NO ☒

21A. ACCIDENT ☐ SUICIDE ☐ HOMICIDE ☐
21B. DESCRIBE HOW INJURY OCCURRED (Enter nature of injury in Part I or Part II of Item 19)
RECEIVED
APR 18 1957

21C. TIME OF INJURY HOUR A.M. P.M. MO. DAY YR.

21D. INJURY OCCURRED WHILE AT WORK ☐ NOT WHILE AT WORK ☐
21E. PLACE OF INJURY (In or About Home, Farm, Factory, Street, Office Building, etc.)
21F. PLACE OF INJURY CITY, TOWN OR RURAL COUNTY STATE

22. I HEREBY CERTIFY THAT THE DECEASED DIED ON THE DATE AND FROM THE CAUSE STATED ABOVE
SIGNATURE M.D. D.O. OTHER (SPECIFY) ADDRESS U. T. Memorial Hospital DATE 4/8/57

23A. BURIAL, CREMATION, REMOVAL (SPECIFY) BURIAL
23B. DATE OF BURIAL, CREMATION, OR REMOVAL 4-14-57
23C. NAME OF CEMETERY OR CREMATORY OAK GROVE
23D. LOCATION CITY, TOWN OR COUNTY BLUEFIELD, W. VA. STATE

24. FUNERAL DIRECTOR DOCKERY-TEMPLE
ADDRESS MORRISTOWN TENNESSEE
25. REGISTRATION DIST. NO. 4
26. DATE SIGNED BY LOCAL REG. 4-18-1957
27. REGISTRAR'S SIGNATURE Mary Chambers

At the time of his death, Dr. Dickason was serving as the President of Morristown College in Morristown, Tennessee. He was hospitalized in Kingsport, Tennessee, where he died in 1957. *Tennessee Office of Vital Records, Nashville, TN.*

Dr. Henry Lake Dickason's final resting place in Oak Grove Cemetery in Bluewell, WV. *Becky Crabtree.*

Dixie Hill Cemetery

The Dunlap family plot in Dixie Hill Cemetery in a clearing surrounded by forest. The cemetery is located near Gap Mills, WV, high on a mountain, not far from the family's farm. Becky Crabtree.

The Dunlap family plot is nestled in the forest high on Dixie Hill near Gap Mills, West Virginia.
Becky Crabree.

Index

Individuals

Businesses and Organizations

Locations

Historical Events

Becky Hatcher Crabtree

West Virginia educator and author Becky Hatcher Crabtree first became aware of Henry Lake Dickason after she and her husband Roger rented a home thirty-some years ago, Cismont, the grand home that Dr. Dickason had built, without knowing any of the rich history and compelling story connected to Dr. Dickason. Learning from neighbors, friends, and former colleagues and students of Dr. Dickason sparked Crabtree's interest in his remarkable career and lasting influence. The more she learned, the more she became fascinated with his life and achievements. Since then, she has researched Dr. Dickason's life extensively.

She was instrumental in installing a West Virginia State Highway Historical Marker in 2016. Seeing the state of disrepair of the Dickason Family Cemetery, she led efforts to fence the cemetery. Most recently, the author spearheaded a work project for a Boy Scout troop from the National Jamboree to clean and reset the tombstones in the cemetery. The Peters Mountain Chapter of the DAR sponsored all three projects.

Becky Crabtree's life work as a classroom teacher and a school principal reinforces her belief that children need to be aware of strong personalities in their communities and in local history. In her historical biographical novel, she shares her knowledge of the life and times of Dr. Henry Lake Dickason in hopes that others may be inspired to overcome obstacles and "to be somebody."

Becky and Roger currently live in Monroe County, WV. Both are proud graduates of Bluefield State College. They have three daughters: Papi Jeanne, Katherine (Katie) Rebecca, and Dinah Dale. At this writing, they also have five grandchildren: Isabel, Elizabeth, Clark, Gabriel, and Rachel.

Merri Jackson Hess

Merri Jackson Hess was born and raised in Atlanta, Georgia, but has lived in the mountains of southern West Virginia for the past 38 years. Her experiences growing up in the South during the Civil Rights movement contributed to her passion for telling Dr. Dickason's story. A retired public school teacher, her knowledge of American history and world events in addition to skills honed by years of teaching students how to research added a great deal to the historical accuracy of this book.

Hess is an avid reader, crafter, and expert cook of all Southern delicacies. She and husband, Tommy, enjoy travel, movies, and the Atlanta Braves. They plan to relocate to historic Charleston, South Carolina to live closer to daughter, Tamara Padgett, her husband Paul, and grandson Rich.

CPSIA information can be obtained
at www.ICGtesting.com
Printed in the USA
FSOW04n0447270917
39054FS